ASH JACKSON

BEYOND TRANS

BEYOND TRANS

Supplementary material for this book including extra multimedia can be found at:

www.ashjackson.com

Copyright © 2024 by Ash Jackson

All rights reserved. No part of this book may be reproduced in any manner whatsoever without written permission except in the case of brief quotations embodied in critical articles and reviews

First Printing, 2024

Dedicated to my Mum and Dad,
My brother Brad, sister-in-law Fran,
and my adorable nieces

You all give me strength even when I'm at my weakest...

FOREWORD BY MATT GLOVER

Ash has been my friend for a long time now. Sometimes people say that it is admirable the way that I work with people like Ash and help them navigate the rollercoaster of gender transition, mental health and life.

While I may have contributed something to Ash's journey, the truth is that most of the time it has been the reverse. My life has faced different obstacles and challenges. I have been accused, harassed, ridiculed and abandoned. Often by people who I thought were friends. But Ash has never wavered in her support or care for me. She has always been the friendly voice on the other end of the phone. The source of groan-worthy jokes that brought a smile in dark times. The companion who never gives up, even when I'm a terrible friend. Ash has known what I've been going through because she has gone through it too. Only a hundred times worse. Maybe a thousand times.

This is the story of one amazing individual. How one person manages to fit so much into so few years escapes me. The different things she has done are intriguing, to say the least, but it's the glimpse into her inner world that makes this story remarkable.
She has inspired me for many years now. Being able to read her story in more detail inspires me more. I hope the story inspires you too.

FOREWORD BY NATHAN REES

I moved from Western Sydney to St Kilda, Victoria in 2020, just before COVID lockdowns commenced. The whole city, indeed the whole world, was turned on its head through public health measures introduced to restrict the spread of the virus. For many, the isolation was very real, but it also impressed on the whole community with the value of togetherness and friendship.

It was during this period that I met Ash Jackson, and over time we became friends. Ash had given me snippets of her life while she was growing up, but it wasn't until I read her manuscript for this book that I realised just how extraordinary her life has been. In the following pages, you will read about her wrestling, television career and her passion for music. You will also read of her deep love for her family and friends. You will read of her experience with fringe groups, and her deep compassion for others.

However, most remarkably, you will read the work of a woman who is laying her soul bare, articulating an extraordinary exercise in bravery. The term "journey" in a personal growth context is overused, but this book outlines the incredible and genuine journey of a trans woman.

No one will read this book and not be moved by Ash Jackson's courage and grace. And, it should make us feel uncomfortable as a society that we allow the brutishness of intolerance that marks too many pages of Ash's book.

The trans debate is complex, and its implications are huge, especially for the individuals involved. For those amongst us who have a black-and-white approach to male/female gendering, I doubt you can read this book and come away without a more nuanced view of the world.

Ash's book is not just a monument to her courage and perseverance, it is also a valuable contribution to a broader debate that demands that we examine our society and its values more closely. In holding this mirror up, Ash has personally made a contribution to public discourse that will, over time, help shift our tolerance dial. Ash's book will help make the world a better place.

FOREWORD BY MATTHEW MUIR
"JUNGLE CAT"

I first met Ash back in late 1999. I'd just made my debut as a Professional Wrestler. As someone who had represented Australia in both bodybuilding and powerlifting, I thought Professional Wrestling was going to be a breeze and I'd pick it up quickly. In short: it wasn't and I didn't. Pro Wrestling was VERY MUCH harder than I thought it would ever be. But I digress. I'd heard a lot about a Victorian Wrestler called "Cobra". Tough. Skilled. Had to be seen to be believed. Pro Wrestlers are not known for "putting over" (praising) their fellow workers and it was high praise indeed that I was hearing. All the talk was right.

I remember vividly a match at the Macedonian Club in Epping where Ash (as Cobra) and Ricky Diamond brought the house down. The capacity crowd on their feet screaming at the conclusion. The wrestler's change rooms were a "curtain sell out". All of the wrestlers watched the match, as best they could from whatever position they could find backstage, and I can remember thinking to myself "There's no way I'll EVER reach THAT level...". Both disappointed in my own shortcomings and stunned at the level of athleticism I had just witnessed, I joined a standing ovation that all of the wrestlers gave both Ash and Ricky as they entered the change room. Ricky was covered in blood and Ash was being carried by a security guard on each side supporting the spent athlete who had just torn the house down. Stunned I looked at Ash... his eyes rolled back into his head. And he collapsed to the floor. A collective gasp went up from ALL the wrestlers... Then Ash stood bolt upright. HUGE smile on his face. And said: "GOTCHA!". We all laughed and took turns coming over to shake Ash's hand. Still the best match I've ever seen live.

Fast forward a dozen or so years and we're in the age of social media. I'm scrolling Facebook one day and the name "Ash Jackson" comes up as a profile. Whether it was me requesting friendship or Ash I honestly can't remember. Either way, we pick right up where we left off, with Ash openly and candidly talking about her transition. After many years of partying and working security within the LGBT community, I'm nowadays described as an ally.

I've always felt protective and supportive of people that we're marginalised. And had the highest respect for people who have fought through adversity. This describes many of my trans friends and certainly describes Ash. She has put her journey and struggle into the public eye for all to see. Her candor was disarming and raised her even further esteem of her character...

We ALL face struggles in our lives. Some face it quietly and some stoically...others like myself turn to self-medication and self-loathing. During a very low patch in my life (just a few years ago) I was at my wits end. Not sure what to do or where to turn and finding myself consumed with self-destructive thoughts I'd never seriously entertained before, I reached out to quite a few people I considered close to me with none returning my communication, except Ash... Her messages were thoughtful and considerate. Showing that over the previous few years, she'd TRULY listened to me and valued me at a level where she'd thought of what could give me hope and ease my mind. All were contained in quickly returned messages and an open invitation to come to Melbourne and stay with her until things got better. I was humbled to the point of silence and honestly moved to tears.

Despite her own struggles and personal demons she still hadn't lost that love or loyalty for her friends. I felt the same way again being asked to write this foreword: Humbled that Ash would ask me. I've always admired her for many different reasons. I'm looking forward to fully reading this book myself so I can TRULY get to know the person I admire so much. Thank you Ash. Honoured to call you my friend...

INTRODUCTION

When I was a kid I dreamed of being famous. I dreamed of playing guitar in stadiums, having crowds singing along to my songs, hearing my compositions on the radio and all the comfort that such a lifestyle would provide: To walk down the street and be recognised. To be so popular that I eventually wouldn't be able to walk down the street for fear of being recognised. I would finally be popular and all the people who had been part of my life would know that I was important. That I was famous. That was when I was younger. As my life progressed and I matured that dream eventually faded. I had played in many rock bands and enjoyed performing, but I felt ashamed and almost embarrassed if someone complimented my playing abilities. I had a lot of pain inside. I was hurting and unable to be how my brain and soul felt inside.

Now as I sit here alone in my apartment with the television on and a nice cold beer in my hand, I await my television premiere so to speak. It is Wednesday the 23rd of February 2022 and in a few minutes a nightly national TV show called "The Project" is featuring a story about me. About my pain. About my loneliness and desperation to find a community that cared for me. Part of me wants to turn it off and lock myself in my room for the next few weeks until this all passes. I don't want this type of attention. I don't want to be recognised. I don't want any part of being famous this way, even if it's just my own "fifteen minutes", as

Andy Warhol once philosophised.

This is not the way I thought my debut would be, I look pathetic. I thought it would be a great feeling, but it's almost embarrassing. I can see myself on the box sitting across from the host Waleed Aly. It's a surreal moment. I don't want this. I wish someone else could be in my shoes and tell my story. But indeed the message is far more important than my lack of confidence and self-esteem.

Gosh, I look so sad. I guess that makes sense because my best friend passed away a fortnight ago. I don't think I have smiled much since. I am still a mess trying to cope day by day with my devastation. There I am on screen talking about the past two years of my life. It all started when the 2020 Covid pandemic began to gain momentum. I think this story might help someone, maybe even myself. But to understand the complete story I will have to tell you, the reader, the whole story... My story.

GROWING UP

I was born on March 25th, 1973 in Melbourne after my Mother went through an agonising fifty-two hours in labour. My parents, Bill and Liz, had been married for three years by then and are still together to this very day. My Mum was quite small in stature at just over five feet tall, but what she lacked in height she made up with in her kindness and love for her family. A lot of people said that I look similar to my Mum with our brown hair, brown eyes and I was lucky enough to have rich, thick hair like her. My Dad was slightly taller than my Mum and had the reverse appearance up top, with very little hair. A very stoic man but he always was the life of the party and had very confident outgoing social skills.

My Pop (grandfather on my father's side) was quite sick in hospital at the same time as my birth and he always said it was the news of having a first grandchild that pulled him through. He was a small man and would shuffle along through his days as a butcher. Of course, I must rely on my parents' memories from this time, which included on average hospital visits every couple of weeks for my first few years of life. I survived having pneumonia four times within my first nine months of life and was indeed a rather sick baby boy. The cause of all this was chronic asthma, something I inherited from my Nanna.

She was a rather quiet lady and even shorter than my Mum, but like my Mum had a beautiful heart of gold, raising my father and my uncle Michael. They were three years apart in age and both had a wicked sense of humour. He was an outstanding tennis player and student of karate while my Dad was an acomplished singer and guitarist.

My brother Brad and his twin Sarah were born three years after my entry into the world. My sister died just after birth and I have always wondered and wanted a sister. Apparently, as an older brother, I was quite mean to the family's newest addition and within his first few weeks of life I pulled back his bassinet bouncer like a slingshot and sent him flying to the ground. Thankfully he survived and as time went on I guess I got used to him being around. As I was almost a carbon copy of my Mum, he was the same as my Dad.

When we were a few years older I remember us in our bedroom thinking what a great idea it would be to see if we could get our "Bionic Man" doll in the dish part of the light hanging from the ceiling. We took turns hurling the plastic figure up higher and higher, sometimes scraping the light and would go collect the doll and pass it to each other over and over again. My last attempt almost worked as I threw the doll high up and we both looked knowing one of us was about to accomplish the feat and in turn be the winner. It got in and immediately the glass fitting shattered and fell. What I didn't realise was that my brother was still under the light and broken glass shards came crashing onto his head. The screams and tears began as I ran to get my mum and we proceeded to cover his cracked bleeding skull with bathroom towels. Then off to the hospital we went where he received many stitches and I was full of guilt and remorse as tears flowed from my eyes and seemed to never stop. It was my fault that I had hurt my brother. As the older sibling I was meant to be his protector and throughout primary school, I was constantly in trouble for beating up anyone who dared pick on him. This would always be the case throughout our lives and although we have had many ups and downs, we always would find a way to get past our troubles.

I think sometime around the age of four or five, I had a feeling that I wasn't happy in my skin. Of course I was happy overall but there was an inner questioning regarding why I couldn't wear stuff that girls were wearing. It was driven home and cemented into my mind very quickly that boys were forbidden to be feminine in any way. Girls could wear what they wanted, be expressive, they were always neat and clean and I wondered what it would be like to be as free as I imagined they truly were. My first early memories of doing anything remotely feminine was at the same age when I clumsily went to my bedroom by myself and painted my toenails in a reddish-pink polish. I was so happy that I had pulled it off and that no one would ever know because boys wore socks with their shoes. I was caught out by my Mum a few weeks later when she went to cut my toenails. She looked quite puzzled as the toddler's naivety in me professed that I had cut my toes running outside in bare feet.

At kindergarten, I would always enjoy playing dress up and would feel so disappointed when we were told to change back into our clothes. I was one of the girls and I temporarily felt free. This led to getting politely reminded that I was a boy and boys don't wear dresses. This made me feel sad. So sad that throughout my primary school years, I would often be told to smile. My annual school photos were a nightmare as the photographer tried to get me to smile. My soul just didn't want to smile. I had been told I couldn't be myself and why then should I pretend to be happy? I dared not ever to divulge my secret for to do so in that day and age meant nothing but hate towards such a child. Probably an exaggeration but that was how I truly felt. This was the beginning of my self-loathing and shame which would continue for many decades to follow.

For the most part, my years at school from age six to twelve were quite happy. Besides being famous at school for not smiling and constantly being told by my teachers "Smile Ashley Smile" and "You won't get anywhere in life if you don't smile", I would say it was a great childhood. My Dad worked the daytime at a bank and my mum worked at the Milk Bar where we lived. At night my Dad would take over while Mum looked after us. I really loved living there and miss those old days of the classic Milk Bar. The bottles of fresh milk with an aluminium lid, plus lollies were one cent and you got to choose from the dozens of containers didplayed in a glass cabinet. Also the milkshakes, comic book section, freshly made sandwiches and hot bread deliveries on Sundays. It was a great time to be a kid.

My parents were extremely hard-working and loving and I consider that one of the most important blessings in my life. My Dad played in several bands every night of the weekend. He played rhythm guitar and sang all the hits of the day from Creedence Clearwater Revival, The Beatles, Kenny Rogers, Shakin Stevens and even some old raspy blues numbers like "Mustang Sally" and popular hits from the fifties to the eighties. I remember looking at him on stage and thinkg "My Dad is famous", not realising that it was just a cover band, but I didn't care. He was MY Dad. Ironically I had no interest in learning music at all, although that would change in my first year of being a teenager. One of his later bands "Oregon" won the "Battle of the Bands" in 1980 and his statue has remained on display in my parents' home ever since, alongside my Mum's many premiership medals for playing basketball.

As a kid, my mum, brother and I would spend a few weeks every summer holiday at Sorrento in a friend's shared caravan. They were golden times spent on the beach, swimming, walking on tracks, discovering little creatures at low tide on the side rocks of the beach, the aquarium with the daily seal show, a visit to the Milk Bar, a car drive over to the back-beach and of course fishing. This was also a time when I noticed the very distinct differences between boys my age and girls my age. I had to wear shorts and they got to wear a pretty swimsuit and I was so jealous. Why was God putting me through this? I thought. I was so confused and sad to be a boy...

In my first few years at St Clare's primary school in Box Hill North, my friends were mostly all girls and I didn't even think anything of it. I just got along with them better than the boys and it was just a beautiful fun time secretly being one of the girls, even though it wasn't the true reality of what was happening. I didn't even think that boys and girls were that different except our uniforms and being gentle was just an inside part of my soul. Of course, secretly I wanted to wear a dress and truly be able to be myself without having the constraints and limits of being trapped as a male which I had to hide at all costs.

My home life at this time was great and we had finally moved out from living above the Milk Bar to a modest house just up the street. Time after school was usually spent with friends coming over and playing until it was dark and we knew it was time to head home. This was typical of life in the suburbs of Melbourne during the seventies and eighties.

Weekends consisted of playing tennis on a Saturday morning then getting home and cleaning the house before Mum got home from her morning shift at K-mart. My uncle Michael taught me how to play tennis from around the age of eight and he was by far the most influential and closest relative outside of my immediate family. We had a major falling out many decades later as I said something to him that was completely unforgivable. As I write this we have not spoken in ten years. I wish I could repair our relationship. I often dream about him and miss him dearly.

Occasionally on a weekend night, we would get a pizza or even fish and chips. I loved these times but I felt lonely for my Mum. Dad would be off gigging in his band and although we would sometimes see him play, I knew Mum missed him as we all did. I would often get sent to bed on a Saturday night and sneak down to the front window out of sight. I just stared out at the street waiting for Dad to come home until I started dozing off and eventually headed back to bed.

Most weekends I would also spend time either visiting or staying over at my Nanna and Pop's home in Clifton Hill. Their Victorian-style house on Gold Street was opposite Darling Gardens, a gigantic park lined with palm trees, swings and even war memorabilia canons and my brother and I loved it. It was only a five-minute walk from the Clifton Tennis Club where I would frequent more and more as I got older and became a better player.

Nanna and Pop loved us so much and would spoil us beyond belief. I didn't think until years later that my mother's parents

(Gran and Grandad) would have found it so much harder to spoil their grandchildren. There were already dozens as my Mum came from a family of ten children and they lived quite further away in Essendon. I loved them all equally but of course, I favoured my Nanna and Pop. In saying that though, I did become a lot closer to my Gran and Grandad later in my life.

My world became damaged in grade three, the year before I would turn ten years old and become a "ten-ager" as my Grandad said. The teacher, Mrs Anthony, who was once a catholic nun in Sri Lanka or India, had a fair dislike for the opposite sex to say the least. She was a very old lady and of course, set in her ways and one of those was punishing boys when they were misbehaving and scaring their minds for life. A school dress would be hanging up on the back wall of the classroom. Her threat was that any boys misbehaving might find themselves wearing it was always in the air. Thankfully no one that I knew of was forced to wear it as a humiliating punishment, but there were much more minor ways for her to torture a young boy's psyche that she would occasionally explore and justify in her twisted ways.

The life-changing moment that would cement many decades of shame and self-hatred was courtesy of her. She would tell me off constantly for playing with the girls and would order me to go down to the quadrangle and play basketball or cricket with the other boys. I didn't want to and would usually just walk away and find something to do by myself. One day I dared to defy her as she ordered me to be like the other boys. I told her "No, these are my friends right here" and she walked away. I presumed I had won and I went back to playing with the girls. Little did I know what was in store for me after lunchtime had finished and we all headed back to our classroom.

I sat down at my desk and I could tell already that she had it in for me as she ordered me to the front of the class. I knew I was about to cop something as her words blurred and all I heard was: "Time for punishment". She pulled out a hair tie and a pink ribbon from her desk drawer and started tying my hair in a silly-looking ponytail of some description. All the kids started laughing, mainly the boys, as she then tied up the ribbon in a bow. I was bright red and crying in embarrassment and tried to take it out only to get a smack from her. An older student came into the room to deliver some type of message and my teacher proclaimed: "Thank you. Please say hello to our new student. Isn't she pretty?" The older girl just giggled as she left the room and then most of the class were in hysterics laughing as I stood there humiliated with tears flowing down my cheeks. From that moment on it was permanently imprinted into my mind to never display any femininity in any way for fear of being ostracised and humiliated again. I stopped hanging around girls and even became somewhat afraid to even talk to them. I buried my soul into a deep dark place and tried to forget my earlier school years. I never told anyone about this until I came out to my church pastor well over twenty years later.

I also became extremely protective of my brother after an event where Eddie, the local street bully, pushed my brother off his bike so hard that he flew onto the road. He was hurt and crying and I continue even as an adult to have nightmares about it. I lost my mind temporarily and chased him onto his property where he locked himself inside his house. I flipped out as I banged on his door and walked around his house banging on the windows yelling "You are fucking dead...I am going to kill you, you coward". He never came out but there was a police car there an hour or so later so my threats must have spooked him quite a bit. Nothing came of the incident, and I hate to say it but if I had got a hold of him, I would have killed him or sent him to the intensive care unit at Box Hill Hospital.

My final years at primary school were spent getting into stereotypical boy things. Watching TV shows like "The A Team" and movies like "Star Wars" and even professional wrestling. So much so that I would get wrestling figures like Hulk Hogan, Rowdy Roddy Piper, The Iron Sheik, King Kong Bundy and a few others for my birthday. I even got a little play wrestling ring for them and would do matches in them.

"Wrestle Mania" each year was an annual event spent at various friends' homes. It was usually the Pang's house where Andrew and his older brother Sam (yes the same one currently on network television) would watch the annual event on a Friday night and head off to play junior tennis the following morning. I initially only began watching wrestling becase Mr.T, who was an 80s icon and Cindi Lauper, were special guests on the event. It was delayed by weeks so no one knew the results, unlike this day and age where every answer to anything is just a click away on a keyboard or mobile phone. I became obsessed with it and wondered if I could one day grow up to be big and strong like the superstars of the wrestling universe. Maybe by then my feelings of wanting to be a girl would have phased out. Maybe I could be a normal member of society one day. Maybe one day I could even be famous.

The amount of shame and self-hatred that I had learned to suppress by now was hidden even deeper in my thoughts that perhaps that yearning of wanting to be a girl had passed. But of course, it didn't. I still had no interest in music, or rather learning about it like my Dad had and was doing. I loved music of course but just listening to it and pretending as every child does that I could sing exactly like anyone. I mean it must be true, that's how it sounded in my head. I loved "The Beach Boys" as there was a revival of their music in the late seventies and I remember the cassette of their greatest hits constantly on repeat while we spent our summer days holidaying at the beach.

As the years passed I became obsessed with "The Beatles" and the movie "Grease". I would still have thoughts as I watched it wondering how lovely it would feel to be so pretty like the girls in the movie. My desire to be a girl would come back each time stronger than before, and I started dressing up in my mother's clothing at any chance I had while the house was empty. I felt amazingly free and would twirl around and even go out to the backyard. I couldn't understand why any boy would want to remain one, they were dirty and rough. It was now obvious it wasn't going away anytime soon, but perhaps I might grow out of it I thought and be normal, but deep down subconsciously, I did not want to. To feel free and comfortable was a fleeting feeling because I knew I would have to put my trousers back on and go back to being a sad little boy.

In the mid-eighties, another life-defining moment happened. I was at my Nanna and Pop's place being babysat while my parents were out on the town for the night to see "Dire Straits" in concert. I think my brother might have already been in bed as I cannot recall him being in the lounge room. I watched an intriguing movie that seemed like it was made just for me called "Second Serve" and was a true story about a man who changed his sex to become a woman. I hadn't heard of anything like that and never dreamed it would be possible. Richard Raskind was an amateur male tennis player and doctor who had a life full of gender confusion. I was so relieved that I was not the only one in the world that was struggling with their gender. I was staring at the screen as my parents walked in towards the end of the movie, as Richard went into the surgeon's theatre and came out as Renee. I remember my folks saying something like "Oh yeah I remember this. They couldn't work out why he was gay".

I didn't even know what "gay" meant at that tender age and it kind of summed up the lack of knowledge in society in differentiating sex (what you were attracted to) and gender (who you felt you were). I knew all of my friends used it almost as a swear word or derogatory term. If they didn't like something they would say it was "gay". I went to bed that night with dread and hope. Hope that there might be a cure for my inner feelings, yet dread knowing that these same feelings are probably not going to go away, and the knowledge that I may have to deal with them someday in the future, just as Renee did.

Some of my better memories of those times revolved around the summer months and school holidays. We would usually end up down the street at the Mortimer's house for a pool party. It seemed like the whole neighbourhood would attend and my family was no exception. We also would go to Lake Eildon on my parents' houseboat. This was in the 80s and long before the huge drought and carp invasion that eventually forced my folks to sell it.

As I finished primary school I found myself in a position that would take my inner feelings to the next level. I completed classes a week or two before Christmas and had the whole house to myself during the daytime. I started to experiment with fully dressing up and putting on Mum's make-up. I would paint my nails and change outfits several times a day. The big adrenaline rush would occur as I stepped out the front door and walked around the house to the back door. It felt so amazingly comfortable that I wished those moments would never end. I would even sit down to go to the toilet which became a habit and something I would do for the rest of my life. Being a girl meant being free without the barriers of being trapped emotionally and expressively. I was in heaven for a few hours every day but would have to go through the tedious task of removing the make-up and putting everything back where I found it, all the while trying not to leave any evidence.

I'm not sure what to make of my earlier years except that I tried to be happy, but I was in the beginning stages of a life of confusion and hell. And that is society's fault, not mine or my family. There was just too much hatred towards being gay let alone being transgender, and for that reason, my life would not ever be a normal one.

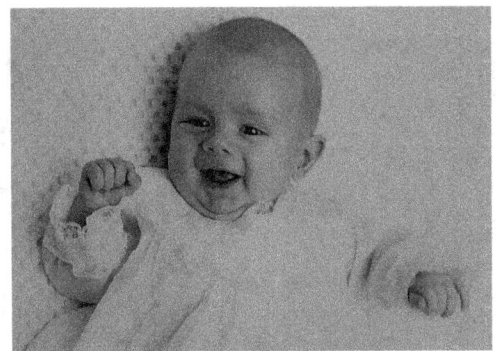
In my Christening gown

Mum and me

Dad and me

At the back of the Milk Bar

My first Redfin at Eildon

My brother Brad and I with Nanna & Pop

CHAPTER 2

HIGH SCHOOL & BEYOND

1986 was a significant year that would again shape the future of the rest of my life, both positively and negatively. The positive side involved my slowly increasing creativity in music as I started to write poetry and song words. I also became madly keen on wanting to learn how to play drums. I begged for a drum kit from my parents but of course, it was a no, and it became a blessing in disguise. In the meantime I made my drum kit with a huge milk-crate frame that supported my tom-toms (shortbread tins placed upside down with rubber stuck onto the bottom which was now the top of each drum), a snare drum with a music stand modified to support it, the cymbals were just the lids of the tins and a bass drum was the inside of the frame and a real kick drum pedal which I borrowed from Joey, the son of Jim Punturere, who was the lead guitarist in my Dad's band. I would practice night and day and it would involve playing along with the "Whispering Jack" concert by John Farnham, "Live in the USSR" by Billy Joel and "Alchemy Live" by Dire Straits.

It was a great foundation for learning how to program drums years later on my Dad's drum machine. I still hadn't discovered the guitar but I knew that music would have a major part in my future. I was songwriting at an incredible rate, although as I look back I now realise they were nothing more than tunes and lyrics that sounded more like nursery rhymes as opposed to my later development as an accomplished songwriter, which would be many years in the making.

It was now time for high school. I was sent to Emmaus College, a catholic co-educational school, which took about ninety minutes via two buses to get to every day. None of my friends from primary school were going there except a few girls that I kind of knew but not very well. It was a rather terrifying experience to be twelve and enter a new world where social status mattered and being called a geek, nerd or dork was about the worst insult anyone could be subject to. Most of the new students already had established friendships with each other from their local primary schools and here I was having to start all over again.

My confidence took a tremendous hit and I declined very quickly into a shy and quiet little boy again. I say "little" because I was probably one of the smallest in the entire year level. I was so small that my necktie was a girl's one as the boys size was way too big. I hated my uniform but admired the girls uniform so much. They just look so clean and neat all the time. I wished that I also could be tidy and confident like they were but it was my secret. I never planned to tell anyone about my inner desires and pretended to myself that it was a phase to grow out of in the next few years.

My weeks each semester would be a similar pattern over and over again. Get up around 7am, eat breakfast, get dressed, catch two buses to school, crawl into my shell during classes, sit by myself at recess and lunchtime, more classes, catch two buses home, do some homework, play by myself in my room with my wrestling dolls and write poetry, bash on my home-made drum kit, eat dinner, repeat the last few steps, go to bed at 8pm and repeat the entire process on the next day. My weekends were spent playing tennis and when I got the chance, I would dress-up!

Oh, I forgot to mention something. The step between knocking off for the school day and getting the bus home: A couple of older students would also wait at my bus stop and they felt it was their duty to bully me mercilessly for the next year. David Beltrami, an arrogant Year 10 student and his big tall buddy decided little Ashley would be their experimental toy. A living breathing punching bag that they could torment every weekday afternoon with things like tripping me over, spitting on me, hitting me, throwing rocks at me and tackling me down with headlocks as I laid down crying in the dirt and grass.

It was a horrific year that destroyed any confidence I had left, and it would haunt me for decades to follow. A few months into my first year of secondary school my Nanna passed away. I am not sure of the whole story other than she had been very sick most of her life with asthma. It was also something I inherited and still have to monitor closely or I may end up in hospital. My Nanna had a severe asthma attack and stopped breathing. By the time the paramedics got there, she was already brain-dead. She was put onto a life support system and it eventually had to be turned off. I was devastated and it just added to my inner hurt that I had already started building a wall around. From then on I would try to stay at my Pop's place in Clifton Hill as many weekends and school holidays as I could manage. Partially to keep him company but it was also a nice break from my horrible school life and I got to practice tennis more often too.

Also that year my Dad and his band called "Lightning Ridge" were cast as the wedding band on a mini-series called "Sword of Honour". It was a movie based around the Vietnam War and showed the human element and after effects that damaged so many brave souls that were later treated worse than animals as they returned home. It starred Andrew Clarke and Tracy Mann. When it got to network television the following year we all sat in front of the TV waiting in anticipation to see Dad on the big screen. It took about thirty minutes and there he was on camera. The band got a few decently lengthy shots but my Dad also got a close-up. I was so proud to tell everyone that my Dad was on the box. The mini-series was amazing and I still watch it from time to time.

The bullying kept going for most of my first year at high school. If I fought back I would just get taken to the ground and would turn blue from being choked. If I walked away I would get rocks thrown at me. One day a rock split my head open and no one helped me, they all just laughed as I walked away with blood trickling down my forehead. On another occasion they pinned me down and thought it was hilarious to rub their crotches into my face calling me a faggot among other things. I hid around a pile of dirt one day where a vacant block was, and yet they still found my new hiding spot. Again back to the headlock and being choked. Then I felt a stream of warm water touching my face. But it wasn't water...it was David's piss.

Some people have told me that writing people's real names might be viewed as defamation, but how it be if it is true? They also said that it's not fair to call others out who have wronged me because maybe that person has moved on with their life. I thought long and hard about it but concluded that "If I am suffering from what they did to me, then who are they to not take accountability, so I have no problem naming and shaming and no fear of being sued. After all, it is what really happened!

The next year they left for the senior campus so the bullying finally ceased to my relief. But the impact of it had destroyed my self-confidence and I would start to burst out bright red with embarrassment when asked a question in class or any social type situation of more than a few people. This would follow and haunt me for years and it would be the main reason that I would turn to alcohol at age seventeen.

My first real crush was around this time. Her name was Jodie Abraham and she was a member of the tennis club where her older sister Lisa and father Rick also played. We were the same age and over the next few years, we would become best friends. We played in the club championship tournament and came runners-up in the mixed section a couple of years after meeting. She first spoke to me on my fourteenth birthday. It was a Friday after school and a bunch of us were practicing. She joined me as we played a doubles match and it was the highlight of my year to say the least. As she left she said "Nice to meet you and happy birthday". We would see each other most weekends and even started to hang out outside of our tennis commitments. She was so beautiful inside and out and I was falling in love. I though that maybe focusing on her would save me from my gender confusion.

Something quite terrifying happened on August the 9th 1987. I found out about it the next day as I sat down in class and the teacher mentioned something about Clifton Hill. My ears pricked up! I was just there last night. I was wondering what happened. During the day I progressively found out and I couldn't believe something so horrible happened next to my beloved tennis club. At around 9:30 on that Sunday night, a lone gunman named

Julian Knight opened fire on Hoddle Street and nearby surroundings killing seven people and seriously injuring many more. I could have been victim number eight. My Mum could have been a victim as well.

I had been playing tennis all afternoon and stuck around to chat with people in the club room that evening. I rang my mum around 8pm and she took the thirty-minute drive to the club to pick me up. Everyone had left and the gates were locked. I sat out the front on a park bench waiting for my Mum in the dark. She arrived around 8:30 and we went home. I later found out that Knight had walked passed that same area around an hour later. This was the first of several close calls throughout my life. I had just dodged a bullet, literally, and fate had decided to give me a very lucky break.

At age sixteen I finally realised that I was not going to ever get a drum kit as a Birthday or Christmas present. I was still writing lyrics and had the melodies in my head, but I couldn't get the music side of them out. My Dad showed me my first chords on guitar and eventually the basics of how to play lead and how to program drum machines and sequencers. As soon as I could play an E and A major chord I wrote my first full song called "Take Every Chance". A very basic song that I recorded with a drum machine and discovered my way of over-dubbing or "ping-ponging" as they call it in the music industry: I would record an instrument on cassette by plugging it directly into my parents' stereo system. Then grab that tape, put it in my Walkman cassette player and feed that audio back into either the left or right-hand side of the stereo, all while recording another instrument of the opposite stereo field. I would do this over and over until I had drums, bass, and two guitars left on one side. Then I would plug a microphone into the opposite side to add the vocal.

As soon as I got home from school my remaining hours were spent practicing, writing and recording. My early influences were quite varied from Buddy Holly with a lot of fifties and sixties music and moving forward to the era of the eighties, which was "my decade" with the glam rock era of Poison and Bon Jovi. For Christmas in 1989, I got my first guitar. A black electric generic copy of a Stratocaster, which one of my idols Ian Moss from Cold Chisel used. It wasn't a Fender like his but it was the same shape and black so I loved it and went to town practicing even harder. My right hand strumming came naturally to me, which would be a challenge for me to understand when I started teaching years later and realising that most of my students had no natural strumming rhythm. I already had a good sense of timing thanks to my homemade drum kit but it was my left fretting hand that was and continues to be a struggle.

I took to music very easily but playing the guitar did not come as easy as I would have liked. Music theory was my next endeavor as I began lessons with a teacher from the local music store. Michelle Nelson introduced me to theory which I picked up very quickly. I remembered a lot of it from my primary school and early high school years when music was a compulsory subject. It was a subject I failed at miserably and believe it or not I failed the recorder in primary school. But now that music was a way of life I somehow remembered little bits a pieces regarding theory and reading music. Michelle taught me the correct way to play rhythm guitar which is a skill unto itself. My foundations were laid down well and I appreciated it much more when years later I would see so many amazing lead guitarists that couldn't hold a groove as a rhythm player.

My school life and weekend life became two separate lives. At school, I was becoming famous for blushing bright red yet on the weekends I was spared that humiliation while hanging out with my awesome friends which Jodie was always the highlight of. As my school life and lack of confidence increased, I found a crossover that meant my blushing condition started to interfere with my weekend social tennis life. I found myself withdrawing even more from any group interactions at the tennis clubhouse for fear of going bright red. I went deep into my music and began to hate all my daily life except my time alone while I was writing. I was such an insignificant person at school that the Emmaus College annual yearbook had comments from our homeroom teacher about every single person except me.

What did I care though? I was going to be a famous musician in the next few years just like Ritchie Valens was at seventeen thirty years prior. When I became famous all the popular people would be so jealous of me. I would finally be important and a lot more important than any of them. Of course, that never happened but a few students from my class including Cameron Baines went on to form a band called "Bodyjar" that would have massive success both here and abroad during the grunge era that was only a few short years away.

My double life was a hard balancing act to be in control of. As far as everyone was concerned, I was an ordinary seventeen-year-old, but at any chance, I would explore my femininity through dressing up and practicing my makeup skills. My dreams often consisted of female scenarios where I was at my wedding in my stunning gown or even things like making out with guys. I would wake up so depressed because the dreams seemed so real. In other dreams, I had a vagina and breasts and again I would wake up knowing this disgusting appendage was still attached to where a vagina should be.

At school, I would sometimes wear tights under my trousers just to secretly feel a bit more relaxed as myself. Sometimes I wore t-bar school shoes which were only allowed for girls in the dress code, only to be sent home after the teacher humiliated me in class saying how pretty they were on me. I didn't care about anyone there anymore and would wag school consistently to go home and dress up while my parents were at work. Returning to school was excruciating getting snickered at and even the girls joking that they could give me a makeover if I liked and then would burst into laughter as my face would go bright red. Again, as I learned before from my previous humiliation ingrained into my brain, I abandoned any pursuit in my femininity and even cut my hair short. Surely this would signal an end to all of this crossdressing and gender-confusing behaviour I thought. I buried myself deep back into my music. It was my escape for now...

My final year at secondary school was a mixed bag of ups and downs. At school, I was becoming increasingly withdrawn and daily life became an extension of that with my depression and anxiety beginning to gradually consume me. I had developed chronic acne all over my face and this was making my life unbearable. There was no escape from it via the multitude of treatments that I tried and the kids at school would call me "pizza face" and "crater face", the worst being Steve Galloway who was a regular all-around bully and jackass. My blushing condition had worsened to the point that I would deliberately fail certain tasks, like doing a talk, just so I could avoid that dreaded feeling of my face burning in embarrassment caused by self-hatred.

If I got too depressed or the verbal insults became too much I would just get up and leave for the day. I couldn't care about any consequences because, in my narrow-mindedness, I thought I was going to be a famous musician within the next few years. All my haters would look at my album covers, see me on television, hear me on the radio and would feel envy and jealousy. I wasn't comfortable in my skin and the wall I was building around myself would stand tall for many more decades. My only solace was at the weekends while playing tennis and staying at my Pop's home. On the odd occasion, I would sleep over at a friend's place or a group of us would make a night of it. Ben Leveson, Andrew Pang, David Bacher, Tom Campbell, Jay Loch and of course my best friend Jodie would occasionally have a Saturday night slumber sleep-over. I remember one very special night Jodie and I snuck out and walked together to the local 7-Eleven for a snack. On the way back the heavens opened up as the rain began pouring. We got stuck under a shop veranda and sat down for a couple of hours chatting about life. It was one of the very few beautiful memories of her that I have never shared with anyone until now.

A few weeks later the Section 1 boys junior tennis team won the grand final and we were all invited for a Saturday night celebration at the clubhouse. Jodie and I went together on the train and shared the Walkman earbuds while listening to "Boom Crash Opera". The writer and member of the band Peter Farnan, who also played guitar, would ironically be one of my songwriting lecturers at Box Hill Institute about fifteen years later. Until that night I had never drank or even thought about drinking alcohol. I didn't have the urge to or even know what it did to the body. I never had plans to ever drink at any time in my life but tonight I would get sucked in via peer pressure, not from my close friends but from the older guys who were drinking up a storm after their sensational victory.

Patrick and Mark, two of the older leaders of the "popular clique", offered me a beer. I had no interest and kindly replied no thanks, but they kept on at me for ages until I agreed to have a sip and taste it. If I thought it smelled bad I now knew that it tasted even worse. I had a few sips and they kept on at me to keep going. I finished the can and threw it in the bin, finally glad that the disgusting taste was over and done with. After ten minutes or so I started to feel quite relaxed and over the next hour my inhibitions faded away and I felt confident to socialise. It was the greatest feeling I had ever felt in my life. I had found the answer to moving on with my life, eliminating the pain and improving my then-benign social skills. It was time for another can and I was feeling great.

Jodie had been drinking too but she was not in a happy place like me. She ended up crying in a corner near the lady's bathroom. I tried to comfort her, but she was inconsolable. My best friend had some issues at home that she was hiding from me. I wanted to hold her and comfort her aching heart. I hoped and prayed that my gender confusion might fade away over the next few years and that I may have a normal life like the rest of society. I wanted that life to include Jodie. I was totally in love with her, and I thought she was my soul mate...

My first ever performance as a musician was in mid-1990. It was the Clifton Tennis Club's annual presentation night and I had put together a band with my close tennis comrades. Ben Leveson was on trumpet, Tom Campbell on keyboard, Sam Schumacher on harmonica and acoustic guitar and myself on electric guitar and lead vocals rounded off with drums and bass on a backing track.

The build up to the night was shaded with some of the popular kids making up rumours that my band was crap and looking back in some respect it probably was. Nevertheless, Jodie came to see our final rehearsal the night before and I was so honoured and excited to have her there supporting us. She was kind of a part of the cool clique and went to bat for us on the night of our gig, contradicting what others were saying and propping us all up for a night to remember. I wondered why a person like me, with serious social anxiety issues, would want to perform on stage and suddenly be the centre of attention. Maybe subconsciously I wanted to face my demons and let myself know that I had the courage to do what most people fear.

We started with some instrumentals followed by songs by Buddy Holly, Daddy Cool, The Rolling Stones and a few others. The audience watched in enjoyment but as soon as the singing started the crowd hit the dance floor and cheered us all on. It was a great success and I knew that music was to be my lifetime obsession. I started mixing my father's band on every weekend night for the next few years as well as doing guest spots playing guitar at some of those gigs. But there was something about to happen that year that would cement my lifetime of bad choices with alcohol.

My Pop passed away suddenly as I was packing my bag at home to go and stay with him over the school holidays. He had a heart attack while in his car and was found hanging halfway out of the door trying to get out for help. My Mum called my name as she approached my bedroom and said she had some bad news, but I already knew somehow. I was crying and throwing things around as I tried to accept that Pop was forever gone. It hit me hard and the next few days were spent in denial until the viewing of his body early in the coming week. My parents and relatives walked into the funeral home for the private viewing, but I couldn't get up and sat in the waiting room for a while. Eventually, I walked in and suddenly broke down hysterically as I saw the coffin from afar. I was bawling my eyes out during those remaining footsteps until I saw his face. He was peaceful and asleep, that's all. The tears stopped for some reason and I felt a soothing come over myself.

I still remember all those times sitting next to him in our reclining lounge chairs, the fold-up dinner trays with fish and chips, watching "Prisoner" and "Cop Shop", him being at my parents' house always kicking the small portable heater while he shuffled along, but most of all I remember that he was a good man and I was seeing why my father had turned out to be such a remarkable man too. I felt shame in knowing that one day I may have to tell my Dad that his first born son was desperately unhappy being a son, being a boy, being a man.

I quit playing tennis not long after that, ironically when I had just been accepted into the Section 1 team. "I was consumed with my music" I told everyone and that was true, but the real reason was that I started shaving my legs and didn't want to be ridiculed when having to wear shorts while playing. During school holidays I was dressing up and wearing makeup for longer and longer periods each day at home. I got my ears pierced and started growing my hair out again. I was still a small person who barely weighed fifty kilograms and would even fit into my cousins' clothes when they visited. I looked at myself in the mirror and would twirl around and daydream that I would one day grow into a beautiful woman. It was irrational and a silly concept to think of in the nineties. Homophobia was alive and well and it is nothing like it is today for younger transgender people who now have a much better chance of transitioning early and having a rewarding life. There was no internet, no information except medical books at the local library and on television gender or sex changes were mocked on such shows as Jerry Springer, Donahue and society overall.

I completed Year 11 and decided to leave without completing the final year of high school. The timing was terrible as a worldwide financial recession was just starting. For the next couple of years, it was impossible to find work, so I had to sign up for Social Security benefits. I also had too much time on my hands and began drinking regularly by visiting my Pop's empty house and raiding his liquor cabinet. I had no thought for the consequences, I just knew it gave me self-confidence. There was nothing that gave me self-worth except for alcohol and I had affirmed my choice that this was the solution to my life.

One night I saw a movie on television that changed my musical direction forever. "Summer Dreams" was a biographical film about the Beach Boys and based on the book "Heroes and Villains" by Steven Gaines. I was fascinated by the rich vocal harmonies and their progression as musicians going from early surf music to dark psychedelic experiments of which even The Beatles became inspired. I went out and bought every record I could find and immersed myself in learning their amazing vocal harmonies. I was always a huge Beatles fan and I started to read up on their writing processes which was similar to Brian Wilson's experiences as he wrote, produced and arranged all the Beach Boys music. Both bands started very young but within a few years were experimenting with drugs and exploring other avenues of composition.

I bought an autobiography of Brian Wilson and also a biography of John Lennon. I was fascinated with the exploration of the mind and had the thought process of: "If they took drugs to write such incredibly innovative music then maybe that is what I need to do". I spent hundreds of hours listening repeatedly to The Beatles' "Sgt.Pepper's Lonely Hearts Club Band" album and the bootleg abandoned masterpiece of The Beach Boys called "Smile" which was preceded of course by "Pet Sounds". I think I had found the answer to brilliant songwriting: It was called Lysergic Acid

Diethylamide, but it was more commonly known as LSD or acid.

By the time I turned eighteen, my life was dramatically changing. I was losing touch with my tennis club friends and Jodie had moved interstate with her father. I started to make new friends with the people that lived in my neighborhood. It was easy to pretend I wasn't shy. All I had to do was drink a few shots of straight vodka and I suddenly had confidence within a short period. My brother Brad had just broken up with his first girlfriend Nicky and as my confidence grew I slowly became friends with her and her best friend Debbie. Within a few months, we had become very close and I was feeling happy that I had actual female friends that I had never really had since my grade three humiliation by Mrs. Anthony. Of course, I had Jodie but she had left and I started to feel much more comfortable being myself around my two new friends.

One night I gathered the courage up and wrote a letter to Nicky telling her about my desire to be a girl. She was okay with it but rightfully concerned about the impact that confessing that to others might have on my life. I remember her telling me that "Guys are not allowed to do anything girly at all" and not to tell my parents for it would break their hearts. I never told Debbie until many years later but together we had fun being silly, hanging out, having slumber parties and occasionally doing feminine activities like painting our nails. They would joke at the way I sat with my legs wide apart and remind me sarcastically that I was a young lady now and should sit like one with my legs crossed. Their friendship made me feel like I was one of the girls again, like in early primary school. I wish I could have transitioned then. I think my life would have turned out better but that old feeling of shame was far too consuming.

Another friend I made during that time lived just around the corner. She was a lovely girl called Sally-Anne Lucas and we became quite close friends and always liked a deep-and-meaningful chat. I never realised until many years later how much emotional pain she was in around that time when she fell pregnant to a guy who was abusing her in different ways. I feel bad looking back and missing the signs because I got on so well with her and wish I had enough courage to confide my gender dysphoria with her. I was fortunate enough to reconnect with her decades later and we are now still dear friends for life. I don't think I have ever known such a lovely, maternal and caring soul as Sal, except for my Mum...

I didn't know it at the time, but I was gradually beginning to show signs of Borderline Personality Disorder. I wouldn't be diagnosed with it until my mid to late thirties and several years after that to understand it. When I first heard the word, I had an uninformed understanding that it sounded like a person with BPD had multiple personalities. It is nothing like that. It means that someone with the condition lives more on the emotional side of life than on the rational side of life. They get upset at small things that most other people don't. They are prone to self-harm like cutting and burning themselves. It can be managed with great success, but I wasn't able to even begin that process until my early forties when I had lost so many friends that I decided to fully accept it and eventually try my best to get help and manage it.

Some of the negative results of my BPD would revolve around my friendships with Nicky, Debbie and Sally-Anne. I would often get jealous if any of them had other plans. That combined with my drinking signaled an end to what were about two of the greatest years of my life. Debbie lived in the spare room at my parents' place while doing her Year 11 study. One day she was crying and I went to comfort her. She said she was upset because I get so jealous when she has her other friends over. I knew I was in the wrong and apologised but her only reply was for me to get out of her room. We never spoke again for many years and she moved to Queensland a few months later to re-start her study and her life. I was a total irrational moron but as long as I was drunk or high I was able to shut any of that pain away.

I took LSD exactly sixteen times in the space of around one year. Most of them were weak and it just felt like I was a little bit high. There are cassette recordings of me that I still have now, while under the influence of acid and writing music. The final time I took LSD it was like going to the moon. The power of it was unbelievable and I started to experience what The Beatles and Brian Wilson would have felt many decades before. In less than an hour I was flying around my parents' house. I was listening to psychedelic music from the sixties and felt at one with the world, as if God had given me a huge glimpse into the realm of heaven.

I remember looking at myself in the mirror and all I saw was my face with a full mask of makeup on. Foundation, blush, eye shadow, mascara, lipstick and my voice sounded girly. I went to the toilet and had a vagina and boobs. It was a million percent so real that I began to panic as others asked where I was. I would be the laughing stock of my friends and I would lose them all if they saw me like this. I was having a very bad trip and it was about to get much worse.

My room was spinning uncontrollably as I began my levitation again, moving around like Supergirl in slow motion. Then it turned to hell. My head exploded like a balloon and I had to rush to the bathroom as my Mum helped me cope with great concern. I threw up a couple of cups of blood and I knew I was in serious trouble. I asked my mum if it was indeed blood and she frantically confirmed that it was. Unknown to me at that time, the LSD I bought at Box Hill Central was cut with battery acid. The junkie-looking guy called Matt sold two of them to me for $50. I found that fact out months later from someone else about the tainted trips, but it puzzled me as to why! I found out years later he had been murdered and that made me feel a sense of justice, after all he could have killed me.

I begged my Mum not to take me to the hospital for fear of getting busted by the police. I laid down on the lounge room couch and rested while Nicky layed next to me comforting me and keeping me calm and relaxed. I was cautious over the next few days and it appeared that my body had managed to get through that disgusting act of deliberate poisoning. I was starting to lose myself, perhaps even losing my mind when I think back to that period, but my booze-fueled days had no concern for anyone but myself. I was now drinking from the moment I woke up until I fell unconscious in my bed later every night. I would even wake up to a bed layered with vomit at times, but I didn't care. I was so unhappy that I wanted to die, I just didn't dare to do it immediately, so I prolonged it over the next couple of years in my alcohol-induced all-day binges.

Waking up consisted of heading to the local liquor store to buy a bottle of the cheapest Port I could find. It cost $4 and was around 20% alcohol in content so that would get me through to midafternoon if I didn't eat too much. Then either another bottle of Port or a bottle of spirits would follow. I would roam the streets and local parks then return home around midnight only to repeat it the following day.

One of my darkest memories that haunts my nightmares even now is the time I hit my Dad. I was drinking heavily and there was a family argument, so I started smashing everything in my room. My Dad came in and told me to calm down and that just set me off in a far worse direction. I tried to leave the room and he stopped me, so I laid into him punching him in the head. He stumbled off stunned and I took off to the local park to drown my sorrows with a shit load more alcohol. When I got home, he opened my door and was teary saying "You've hurt me". Those words and that event are evident even now with the night terrors and horrific nightmares I have every night of my life. My dreams are far worse than any horror movie or realistic mondo-style documentary footage you could ever see. I visit HELL every night when I fall asleep. If my Dad ever reads this I am not sure any apology will suffice, but please know how ashamed I am to have ever hurt you in any way in my life and all I have ever wanted was for you to say you love me and are proud of me.

The incident with my Dad did nothing but add another layer to the wall around my emotions. A wall that trapped my absolute self-hatred for myself and a wall that no one could penetrate. I was never going to let anyone inside my head ever again. I had hurt long enough. My soul was in so much pain. So one night when my parents were out, I picked up a broken piece of glass from a picture frame of Jesus on my wall that I had just smashed in anger and, in front of my brother, I slashed my wrists...

My brother and friends tried to cover up any evidence of my cry for help, but even though I was wearing a long shirt the next day, my parents noticed the marks on my wrists and were adamant I see a psychologist. I saw one for a few sessions but I just told a bunch of half-truths and never divulged my true inner feeling that I was transgender. I wasn't ready to hit rock bottom yet as I had even more baggage and self-loathing to accumulate in the next few years. I still had an undeniable passion for playing music and eventually, my drinking slowed down in anticipation of forming my band. My brother and I had finally started getting along and I wanted to form a group with him in it, just like Brian Wilson did with his brothers in The Beach Boys.

On one social security payday, I spent my entire allowance on buying a second-hand drum kit for my brother because we had started jamming some time before and he was hitting the keyboard note-pads as drums with the synthesized sound patch of a drum kit. Finally, I could start to form a band of my choosing. Me on lead guitar and vocals, a local neighbor Jason on rhythm guitar, my brother Brad on drums and a sequenced click track with a bass guitar in the background. As we progressed and jammed I noticed Brad had impeccable timing. He didn't do any flashy drum rolls but he had the most solid consistent beat I had ever heard. I must confess that as far as timing went, my brother was a gun.

Over the next few months, we brought in a bass player and a rhythm guitarist. We managed to get some gigs playing at birthday parties and every Friday night we would play at the Red House/City Hotel in Johnson Street, Collingwood. We got paid zero but we didn't care, it was all about the fun of being on stage. Also at that time I resumed my role as the sound engineer for my Dad's band and was still writing music every day.

In 1996 I returned to full-time study at Collingwood TAFE doing a "Foundation in Music" course. I was excited to get weekly guitar lessons from Jack Pantazis who was a good friend of my first guitar teacher Michelle. It was my first exposure to jazz music and I found it fascinating. We had classes in a broad range of topics including theory, African percussion, ear training, instrument masterclasses, concerts and a weekly performance in front of my peers. I now had a Sammick brand electric guitar which was designed by Valley Arts. I got it because my idol Jack Jones from the band "Southern Sons" used a real Valley Arts guitar, plus it had a whammy bar so I could do all that crazy "Van Halen" type playing. I saw Jack do a guitar clinic when he was twenty years old. I was blown away that someone so young could be so talented, not only as a virtuoso guitarist but also as a world-class singer.

My brother and I saw Southern Sons' last-ever gig around that time at the Universal Theatre in Fitzroy. They may have been only fifty people there as they had lost some traction in popularity due to the grunge movement, but it was one of the most incredible and loudest gigs I had ever seen. Phil Buckle played rhythm guitar all night which was a surprise as he is a killer lead player like Jack. Peter "Reggie" Bowman had left the band by that stage which was disappointing because he added such an ambiance to the overall sound of a band with three guitarists. Geoff Cain was as solid as a rock on bass and as always Jack was flawless. My mouth was left open in utter awe at the talent he possessed and being only two years older than me. The encore started with a drum solo by Virgil Donati followed by a bunch of cover songs and of course their big hit "Heart in Danger".

Around the early part of that same year, my parents got pay TV. All of a sudden I was exposed to so many shows both old and new. One day I saw a wrestling show and it featured all the old classic wrestlers from the eighties that I was a fan of but had forgotten about, plus it was presented in a way that seemed almost realistic. I became interested in wrestling again and would watch WCW (World Championship Wrestling) weekly on a religious basis. I thought it was so cool that they had Hulk Hogan, Randy Savage and Ric Flair plus exciting new wrestlers who were a lot smaller in stature but showed a new athletic element to the sport. My new favorite was Chris Benoit as he reminded me of a smaller guy I had seen as part of the British Bulldogs, namely the Dynamite Kid. The resemblance in wrestling style was uncanny, so explosive and intense, and I would obsess over it during the next part of my life which was only six or so months away.

I dropped out of my music course around the halfway mark. I felt very guilty because my Dad paid upfront for it. I just cracked it one day at a rehearsal because no one had learned their parts to an instrumental I had written to debut at the next performance in front of the more advanced students.

I was still drinking a few times a week but on a day in late November I woke up to watch a wrestling pay-per-view at around 11am (time difference with USA). I don't know how but I decided to stop drinking and never take drugs again. I wanted my brain back. Wrestling might save me from being transgender and I might even become famous. I was excited and started lifting weights and studying wrestling in slow motion. Looking back I feel that I was just fooling myself as all I experienced for the next five years was daily pain and a further build-up of self-hatred.

My brother was a regular patron at "Stylus Nightclub" and he got talking to the exhibition boxing promoter there named Jim Demirov. My brother mentioned how much I was into wrestling and Jim gave him the number of a trainer for me, although he also stated it's a very tough industry and they don't let just anyone train. I got the number towards the end of the year and discovered that the trainer was a veteran wrestler from the old Festival Hall days named George "The Hitman" Julio.

Mum preparing the Christmas table

My amazing parents, Bill and Liz

My first ever gig

Nicky, Sally-Anne & Debbie

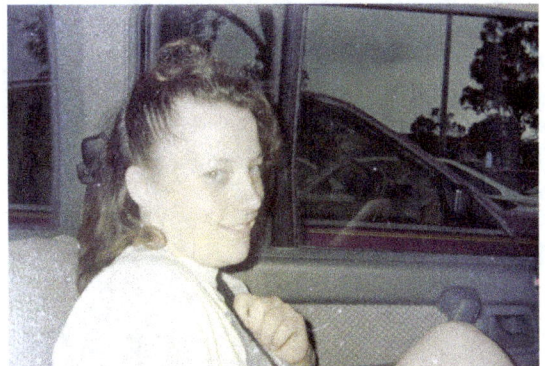

Sally-Anne

Debbie, myself & Nicky

Holding Sally-Anne's baby, Mark

With my parents on my 21st party

My favourite uncle, Michael

Steering my parent's houseboat at Lake Eildon

Dad with his vintage Fender Strat

Keep practicing!

CHAPTER 3

WRESTLING

In January of 1997, I rang the number that Jim Demirov had given to my brother to pass along to me. George picked up and I said I wanted to learn wrestling and he said to come and try it next Wednesday morning. I didn't realise it at the time but the pro-wrestling business in Australia was closed off to the general public. You couldn't just call up a school and pay to learn, which ironically is what it would turn into several years later. The business side of it was oosely controlled by elements of the Mafia and they would sometimes let people try out if they knew a contact, but most tryouts resulted in that person quitting.

I made the trek from Box Hill to George's home in Sunshine North via public transport which would take between two to three hours. I probably could have driven but I was still trying to cope with the PTSD of a serious car accident I had when I was twenty one. I hit the brakes while I lost control in the wet and of course, it made it much worse. I remember seeing cars only metres away from me and I saw my life flash before my eyes. The front passenger side was crushed right up to the middle of the car, if I have had a passenger they would have probably died and I would have gone to prison for drunk driving.

My head was split open and I was eventually taken to hospital smelling like a brewery. I think the police might have been on their way there too, and I knew if I had a blood test from the staff that I would be in big trouble. I asked a nurse if I could go to the toilet and she said "Yes but be quick to return". I snuck my way out of the hospital and walked home taking a bunch of back streets and parks. So I didn't get charged with drunk driving and had dodged another bullet so to speak. It gives me great shame to admit that it took another twenty or so years of drunk driving until I finally got caught. I estimate it to be in the thousands, I say that with absolute disgust and hatred and it is something I can never forgive myself for.

By the time I got a bus, two trains and walked forty-five minutes to George's training gym I had asthma so I needed to stop off at a park next to his house and inhale some Ventolin. I rang his doorbell and he let me in through his gate. "The Hitman" was shorter than me, probably in his early sixties, had muscles on muscles and looked like the real deal. I had trouble understanding his Maltese accent and he looked at my skinny little 57 kilogram frame and asked "So you want to be a wrestler?". Of course, I said and we both got into the wrestling ring.

He taught me the lock-up starting position which he referred to as the "referee hold". It took a few attempts to get it and we locked up as he pushed me onto the ring ropes. Holy shit I thought, these are not ropes. They are steel cables with garden hosing around them and it hurt like hell. He said "You ready?" and I nodded. Instantly he tripped me and my body slammed onto the canvas floor. My head hit the ring and I instantly realised how "real" professional wrestling was.

We kept training for about an hour with a lot of breaks. I couldn't believe how hard it was. On TV it looked so easy, it looked like fun. The only way I can describe the athletic endurance needed would be if you played basketball and never stopped for a break, but kept falling hard over and over again and were not allowed to stop and rest. I thanked George and took my very sorry and aching body back home, with huge canvas burns on my elbows and I felt disappointed that all my aspirations since I was a kid were not going to come true.

Wrestling was as real as anything any top athlete goes through. It was being a stuntman going out to entertain an audience, but only having one take on each stunt as opposed to being filmed for television with multiple takes. I didn't return for about a month but when I called him again he agreed to give me one last chance. I found out years later that George only let me come back because I was honest with him in describing how hard it was, plus I think he saw that I had the heart for it.

When I returned for my next session I felt much more ready. I had been lifting weights at a local gym, running every day, practicing falls on my bed mattress and also mastering the referee hold (locking up) with my Dad. I had put on a few kilograms and as soon as George saw me he smiled and felt my trapezoid muscles. He probably also thought I was crazy because there were no sixty-kilogram wrestlers at all anywhere and he knew my body was going to feel the pain much worse than the bigger "real looking" wrestlers.

It took almost a full year of training for me to become ready for my first match in public. I was and have always been initially a slow learner at everything, but once it all clicks I excel very quickly. I was training at George's regularly and in the first few months he would torture me. I would scream in agony as he taught me the concept of real grappling: how to do it for real and how to imitate the same move without hurting your opponent. George told me about the honour of "kayfabe" which meant you never tip the public off that a wrestling match is an organised form of sports entertainment. It became a sacred oath to me but one that would be shat upon by others only a few years from then, thanks to WWE kingpin Vince McMahon.

As the months went by so too did my training schedule as it increased to twice a week for in-ring training, three times a week at my local gym and every Monday and Friday night taking adult gymnastics classes, then just before Christmas George gave me the news that I was ready and my first match would be next month against my new training partner Austen Young. I needed to organise my outfit and a wrestling name. It took a week or so to come up with my character "Cobra" and I thought it was a decent gimmick being so small, yet sneaky, quick and calculated.

It wasn't until I stepped into the dressing room at the Reggio Calabria Club in Brunswick on January 17th, 1998 that I finally realised the brotherhood and sisterhood of the industry. Psycho Kid Thunder and Ricky Diamond were chatting to each other and laughing about life. I had seen them wrestle a few times and it looked like they legitimately hated each other. Mario Milano was chatting with Con Iakavidis, Bully the Brawler and Wayne Starr.

I was introduced to every person in the room and shook their hand as requested by George. In the wrestling business you must shake hands very softly, because using a firm grip indicates that you are a rough worker and every wrestler wants to be assured that you are a light worker while putting their life in your hands. A "light worker" means that when you do any wrestling move your application against your opponent is so relaxed that you are barely connecting and it's up to your opponent to "sell" that move realistically. There are exceptions to this skill such as hitting in certain areas extremely hard that are deemed safe to do so like the upper back.

I had a chat with the commentary team of Peter Farry and "Mean" Gene Gatto. The promoter Sam Rossi introduced himself as we sat down to get dressed and warm up for the opening match of the evening. Austen and I had been practicing for a few months and had several "spots" worked out, but for the most part, every match back in those days was improvised, which hence was why I trained for almost a whole year. "Spots" are a series of combined moves that show off your individuality, character and signature finish. The winner of the match is pre-determined but if you think it's all just fake pantomime, I can assure you that it is as real as any high-contact sport.

The wrestling ring is similar to a boxing ring. The flooring is made up of several large boards that all link in together and sit above several steel beams, then covered with a piece of very thin foam or carpet, and topped off with a tightly fitted canvas mat. The ropes are industrial steel cables similar to electrical wires that hang between electricity poles, tightened up to make them springy and covered with rubber hosing. Underneath the ring is a huge spring in the middle that lets the floorboards move up and down slightly to somewhat lessen the impact when you fall.

I was extremely nervous as I walked out to the ring. The crowd laughed at how small I was at only 64 kilograms but my muscle tone was quite defined. I remember my first bump in the "real" ring and it felt like concrete. The training ring at George's had extra gym mats which made the impact more bearable, but the falls in this one were devastatingly painful. It's a ring made for people around the 90 kilogram mark not a tiny lightweight like me. The match went to plan: a time limit draw and we got booked again for the following show next month. I felt like I had no place in this industry, I just couldn't toughen up enough or improve at a steady rate. It would be hard to imagine that in just over a year I would be one of the top wrestlers in the country.

That next show in February I saw probably the greatest and purest hardcore match I had ever seen. It was so realistic I thought that Ricky Diamond and Psycho Kid Thunder were legitimately hurting each other. Over the following weeks I discovered that they were very good friends and around the same time I started training with Ricky Diamond, a second-generation young wrestler and a new high-flying lightweight called Chucky. They worked me relentlessly at Julio's gym and I think they were testing me to see how much heart I had and how badly I wanted it. When I look back now I honestly feel it was just another escape from reality, like drinking had been. I felt I was not worthy of being happy, so the dark side of my soul felt I deserved to be in pain, mental and physical, but under it all, I was an emotional wreck.

My next match was held at a new venue called the I.C.K.A Club in East Keilor against another new wrestler called Andy Wishbone. He was a very accomplished drummer in real life, playing in many of Melbourne's top bands over the years. His real name was George Kristy but within a couple of years, he would be one of the biggest stars in the industry as his flamboyant wise-cracking alter ego called "Screaming Lord Lush". We would often train together and call each other on the phone for a couple of hours chatting regularly. His wrestling skills were rather limited but when he got a hold of a microphone there was no one better. He was always cheery and as funny off-stage as he was on.

I felt such a deep sadness when I learned of his suicide in 2014 after he left the wrestling business in pursuit of becoming a famous musician. His band opened up for legendary guitar virtuoso Steve Vai while he toured Australia. He was an all-around great friend but hid his demons way too well for any of his friends to even suspect something was wrong. His story back in 1998 wasn't over by a long shot as he would be an integral contribution to the second wave of Australian wrestling (since the glory days of the 1970s at Festival Hall) which would see us perform several nights a week to regular crowds ranging from four hundred to well over a thousand patrons at every single event.

Once a month a group of us would travel up to Sydney to wrestle on a Sunday afternoon show. We would have shows on a Friday then Saturday night in Melbourne, get in and carpool for twelve hours and arrive in Sydney early morning. Do the afternoon show, carpool it back to Melbourne overnight and go to work on a Monday morning. This is where Ricky Diamond met Amy Action and they went out for the next six or so months. They formed Australia's first supergroup of villains called "The Cult" of which I was the last to join alongside Bulldog O'Reily and Screaming Lord Lush. Together we wreaked havoc on each show, running in to save each other and cheating when the referee was preoccupied. We were a gang that seemed to be somewhat of a highlight during each show and the crowds continued to build every week as the storylines became much more commercial.

Wrestling was going through a massive change overseas and we, the young and new wrestlers, were eagerly learning as much of the new hybrid of styles that we watched from pirated overseas video tapes. There was a divide in wrestling beginning to take shape. There were always the big muscle-bound monsters, but we smaller wrestlers began incorporating a faster pace influenced by lightweight athletes from Mexico and Japan. We were heading in new directions and the crowds were loving our efforts, often with us doing the stand-out matches of every event. With that came a lot more danger as we often flew over the top rope and landed on our opponents outside of the ring with no padding, only a cement or hardwood floor.

The internet was still in its early days and as I joined online forums I got to know two potential wrestlers from Adelaide who made videos doing crazy moves against each other in their backyards. Brett "Jag" Hartley-Jackson and Shannon "Havok" Mills became two great friends online and we would often exchange videos through the mail. Jag would eventually go on to become one of the top wrestlers in the world and became a trainer at the WWE about fifteen years later. I organised their first few matches in Melbourne and they were always technically miles ahead of anyone else on the show. They had found a trainer named Col Devaney and they set up their own wrestling company in South Australia which some of us Melbournians would bus over to fill in the card every month.

My first ever time at a nightclub was a result of being booked for a wrestling event called "Metromania" organized by Chucky and featuring Ricky Diamond, Amy Action, Bulldog O'Reilly and "Livewire" Johnny Parks, a Perth wrestler who had trained and wrestled in the United States. He was ripped and full of muscles and was the only participant who fitted the traditionally accepted image of what a wrestler is. I got a lift in with Bulldog and had pizza on Bourke Street before heading up to the Metro nightclub.

It was going to be a very long and late night with matches planned hourly from midnight until four in the morning. I had to start work at nine so I was unsure how I would get through it all and hopefully not show up to work with any injuries like a black eye which had happened previously.

My match against Chucky was sometime after midnight and we went all out, throwing each other off the stage and onto the dance floor where patrons couldn't believe their eyes as we hit each other to the point of it being almost as real as any street fight. We also used a table outside of the ring and Chucky dived off the top rope and went through the table as I moved at the very last second. I came back after losing the match pretty sore but proud of what we had accomplished and the new precedent we had set for the Australian lightweight wrestling division.

The final match of the night was a Battle Royal, an event consisting of about ten of us in the ring at the same time, where being eliminated was done by being thrown over the top rope to the outside floor area. My old training partner Austen wanted to "juice" for this one but had never done it before so Ricky Diamond agreed to do it to him. The term "juice" means using a tiny piece of a razor blade and slicing it across your forehead to add more realism for the audience as blood trickles down across a wrestler's face. I never understood why wrestlers did that when the public, for the most part, thought it was fake blood anyway.

During the match, I was battling with various participants and I turned around to see Austen's face smothered in blood. It was pouring out and I was extremely concerned for him as Chucky and I arranged to get him out of the ring quickly for medical attention, all while making it look like he had been eliminated. The battle continued and somehow I ended up the winner of the lightweight title belt. It was Sherrie Sinatra's women's title belt that we borrowed but no one knew any different. I got cheered and booed equally and could tell the crowd wanted the big guy Johnny Parks to win and not a scrawny little high-flying newbie.

As I returned to the locker room backstage there was a paramedic tending to Austen. Ricky had accidentally juiced way too deep across the main artery at the top of the forehead. Blood was pouring out like a tap and Austen was looking extremely pale from the loss of blood. He was taken to the hospital and received a lot of stitches. I felt it a bit in poor taste that Chucky would sell VHS copies of the show with Austen's bloodied face as the main picture on the front cover but controversy sells and Chucky, who was never shy to offer an opinion, was quickly becoming rather unliked amongst the wrestling community. His brashness in the face of an industry that was run by older legends, combined with his young age, made him not well appreciated by the experienced wrestlers and promoters. I liked him though and we trained so often together that we became each other's favourite opponent.

My first concussion was received a couple of months later. I was booked to wrestle Austen on his first match back since the Metro incident. One "spot" involved him smashing my head into the turnbuckle and hanging on to my hair as he ran me head-first into the opposite turnbuckle. That was the plan but he ran and threw my head so hard and fast into the opposite turnbuckle that I completely missed it and went into the steel pole and blacked out for a second or two. I didn't know it at the time but it started a chain reaction of concussions over the next couple of years.

By this time I was signing autographs and was somewhat finally "famous" in the Australian wrestling world. It felt great and I felt like an important person and even thought perhaps that my gender issues were fading away. The rest of the year saw me do a few more matches that climaxed at the "December to Remember" show where we hit a record crowd of around 800. It was "standing-room only" for more than half of the audience and we all had a feeling that wrestling was having its second coming since its gigantic following in the seventies. I said farewell to 1998 with an award as the "Australian Rookie of the Year". But that was only minor in comparison to where the next twelve months would take me.

My fitness level was becoming extremely high with only a few percent of body fat. Training every day became the norm for me whether it was in the ring, in the gym, gymnastics, or researching new moves and trying to understand the psychology of what makes a wrestler great as opposed to where I currently was. I hadn't sipped alcohol in about two years so there was a positive spin to all my inner torment of wishing I could be a woman. Looking back I would say that I just replaced an addiction to the booze with an addiction of self-harm through hurting my body. Nothing had changed inside me, it just became suppressed with the feeling of being a somewhat pseudo-celebrity in the wrestling world down under.

My last match at the "December to Remember" event was a real breakthrough and earned me a match in the main event at the first show of 1999. A tag-team match with Ricky Diamond against Chucky and the main superstar at the time, Psycho Kid Thunder. This was a difficult match due to my over-training. I had hurt a disc in my lower back and was seeing a local chiropractor twice a week. I was in serious pain during the entire match but took some strong codeine and anti-inflammatory tablets so I could at least get through it and take a few weeks off to recover. The next morning I could barely move and became bedridden for a few days but was fortunate enough to get time off from my job.

Training with the legend George "Hitman" Julio

The Cult, Aussie wrestling's first supergroup

Psycho Kid Thunder

Mean Gene & Peter Farry

Chucky -v- Cobra

Jungle Cat

Pics courtesy of Adam Kember

CHAPTER 4

COBRA, LOCO, CONCUSSIONS & CARNAGE

April of 1999 was an evolving time as everything just started to come together and feel a lot more natural. We were doing two or three shows a week as well as Chucky setting up a series of new shows under the company name of JKW (Junior Kickstart Wrestling), featuring all young and more high-flying talent such as Ricky Diamond, Screaming Lord Lush, Man in Black, Bulldog O'Reilly, Psycho Kid Thunder, Skyhawk, Chucky's girlfriend and manager Tash, Austen Young, Blade Runner and myself.

There were a few important events around that time including my first "suicide dive" in a match against Blade Runner, which received a standing ovation. A suicide dive is where a wrestler runs fast across the ring and dives out onto their opponent who is outside the ring. It would become my signature move, but also caused a lot of my injuries. My main memory of that match at the I.C.K.A Club was Screaming Lord Lush with "The Cult" running in to save me as Blade Runner was about to get the victory, and Lush kneeling to check how I was with the biggest grin on his face saying "Man you are crazy!". The next day Chucky had a show organised at the Queen Victoria Market. We both went through a table from the ring apron onto and breaking the table and hitting the cement ground. I remember Criss Fresh from a fan group called "The Asylum" proclaiming out loud: "There are people here laughing and saying it's not real, well have a look at that. Let's give them a round of applause". We had done something never done before in Australian wrestling, and although I was in tremendous pain, I loved that I was finally somewhat famous...well at least to Aussie wrestling fans!

A week or so later Chucky and I were the opening match for a new venue at the Macedonian Club in Epping. We had a few good spots planned out from our training session the night before at "The Dungeon" in Richmond. It was a martial arts gym where the owners allowed us to train up-and-coming wrestlers in the basics. The head trainer was Ricky Diamond but myself and Chucky were there nearly every other week to help. The match set a new standard for Australian lightweight wrestling with high-flying moves never seen before in our country. We even went a bit hardcore with Chucky suplexing me onto the hardwood floor and the use of chairs as weapons. We had stolen the show again and the ego of both of us felt rather proud even though I was hurt quite badly.

Around the same time, Chucky had booked a few monthly shows under his promotion's banner of JKW at a venue called the High Ryder Saloon. It was a pub along King Street, which at the time was notorious for gangland violence including an incident with Jason Moran and Alphonse Gangitano. These were Friday night shows in front of a heavily intoxicated audience consisting of three to four matches followed by the latest American pay-per-view streamed on a big screen.

Chucky and I had now established a reputation as two of the best lightweight wrestlers in Melbourne and a feud had developed over many months preceding our two hardcore matches at the King Street venue. We were so believable that most fans thought we hated each other in real life but we were actually very close friends. The first match in late April almost destroyed me. It was a "Falls count anywhere in the pub" match, so we did our usual moves but out on the hardwood floor as opposed to the spring of the wrestling ring. After I took a power-bomb on the floor, I hit the back of my head and knew I was in deep shit. I continued through the pain and copped two suplexes again on the wooden floor, but I did manage to do a moonsault (backflip) from the back of a couch. I ended up unconscious and getting pinned on the pool table. Most of it was a blackout and although I was in horrible pain, I felt good about myself. It was a feeling that "I am such a shit human being that I deserve this and I am prepared to die to void my inner emotional pain".

The re-match the following month, we introduced the use of barbed-wire in another hardcore match. Chucky brought along a folded-up chair wrapped in the wire and I used it to win the match by giving him a "Frankensteiner" from the top turnbuckle onto the chair. Again we took the match all around the pub and got near the exit where the crowd started chanting for us to go out onto King Street to fight. The owner Trevor blocked our path and unfortunately that was the last wrestling event ever held there. Trevor also ran a strip club upstairs and the guys would frequent it after the show. I felt ridiculously uncomfortable as the boys were turned on by the ladies while I secretly wanted to be a lady.

In July myself and Chucky caught a bus overnight to premiere our Melbourne wrestling style for the AWF (Australasian Wrestling Federation) at the Blacktown Civic Centre in Sydney. It was a new company started up by a wrestler called TNT (Greg Bownds) and a rather wealthy financier Rob Jones. Word had been getting around the wrestling industry in Australia about our previous matches and we didn't disappoint anyone as we had a match that would be later voted "Australian Match of the Year" by internet fans. I also got to meet a celebrity called Vulkan from the TV show "Gladiator" as he faced off against TNT in the main event later that night.

One of my favorite matches happened around that same month, again at the Macedonian Club in Epping for the NWA (National Wrestling Australia) promotion run by Jim Demirov. It was a semi-main event and was for the Hardcore Championship against title holder Ricky Diamond. He had a bunch of great spots planned and he even brought along the kitchen sink, literally. The end of the match had me getting suplexed from the top turnbuckle right through a table that ironically we had put together earlier that day with the help of my Dad. I even got paid a bonus of twenty dollars which brought my pay up to seventy dollars. I accidentally gave Ricky a concussion during the match by smashing his head with a frypan. I hit him so hard that the handle broke off.

The AWF called again with an offer I couldn't refuse. They would be touring the East Coast over a month with a show called "Psychotic Slam" featuring Australia's best wrestlers and international talents Super Dragon, Gothic Knight, Chris Candido with Sunny, Marty Janetty and Sabu. I could not believe my good fortune to be included as one of Australia's best and it took about one second to agree to such a privilege. OMG, I was becoming famous now and this tour would cement my position and future financial opportunities within the industry. I was twenty-six and famous, broke as a joke but I had accomplished something barely anyone in society could...I was fucking famous! Well, kind of...

A week before the AWF tour I had a very serious concussion. The JKW crew were booked in Adelaide, South Australia at the Thebarton Theatre for the first major wrestling show there in decades. It was a sold-out event with around 1,800 patrons selling at around the $40 mark per ticket. It was a tournament featuring myself, JT Robinson, MIB (Man in Black), Steve Frost, Chucky, Tash, and local talent Matt Rott, Larry Rhino, and Mad Max Miller who would later become one of Australia's finest actors, appearing in the TV shows "Home & Away", "Underbelly" and "Gallipoli" as well as movies such as "Wolf Creek", "Animal Kingdom" and "The Line". Also flown in was TNT from Sydney to fight Chucky in an extra non-tournament main event.

The majority of the crew from Melbourne had to take an overnight bus to Adelaide while Chucky managed to get a flight seeing that he had organised the event alongside the local promoter Adrian Manera. As we waited at the departure Greyhound bus depot, Chucky informed us that the previous week the venue in Adelaide had been shot up by the local Mafia in response to our event "invading" their city without a pay-off. In those days wrestling was somewhat governed by the Mob and Chucky was not well-liked, especially in a new location interstate.

When we arrived in the afternoon at the venue it looked huge and it was hard to believe it was sold out. The downside was the ring...it was a boxing ring with no spring under the floorboards and in a few hours it contributed to a concussion so bad that I would never fully recover. My first and only match of the JKW tournament was against JT Robinson from Sydney. I had been corresponding with him over the internet and he was instrumental in getting myself and Chucky booked for matches at the upcoming "Psychotic Slam" tour.

We had some great spots planned but my small athletic body was not ready for continuous bumps on a boxing ring. There was no give whatsoever and I received a few devastating knocks to the back of my head. The "show plan" was to have me eliminated by Chucky interfering in the match and later in the night challenge Chucky to a hardcore match for my revenge. I was too badly concussed to follow through with the original idea so the plans had to be altered. Jag drove me to a doctor's clinic but, upon seeing the dozens of people waiting, I decided to just go back to the dressing room at the venue and rest. It was by far the worst concussion out of many more to come, I truly felt as if a part of my brain was damaged that night. Yet I still had so much self-hatred that I felt I deserved it and in less than a week I would have to "man up" and go on tour with Australia's best and the incredible talents from America.

In August of 1999, we once again caught the overnight bus to Sydney and headed over to the AWF headquarters in Mount Druitt. We were pretty excited about being the only two Melbourne wrestlers to be asked to go on tour. We were being accommodated for back in the city at the infamous Kings Cross at a five-star hotel called the "Park Royal". At around mid-afternoon the entire talent roster boarded a chartered bus to head to the first show in Newcastle. I couldn't believe it, suddenly I was on board with Sabu, Marty Janetty, Vulkan, Chris Candido, Sunny (aka. Tammy Lynn Sytch), Super Dragon, Gothic Knight, Jason Helton, TNT and others. Sabu suddenly lit up a joint and ended up arguing with the driver while Chris Candido and Sunny took over the onboard bathroom shooting up various substances. Marty Janetty and Vulkan kept joking with me calling me a "little Eddie Guererro" because of my mullet haircut, the same as Eddie's who was a world-class talent working in WCW at the time.

I sat next to Super Dragon (Danny Lyon) and we planned out our match for the night. I wasn't used to planning an entire match. All I had ever done was plan the start, a few "spots" and an ending while everything else was improvised on feel. The match had good potential to be a great high-flying opening bout, but I wasn't ready for the stiff style of Super Dragon. He was kicking me full-on and I was not ready for such a harsh beating. I always tried to work as light as possible while making it look realistic but barely touching my opponent. He was doing a shoot-type Japanese-influenced style and I came out of the match badly concussed again. I was so badly damaged in my head that I had to return home the following night. I was disappointed but I didn't know this was the beginning of my downward spiral from being one of the best in Australia to having constant injuries and potential brain damage. Chucky continued on the tour but I was seriously considering leaving the industry. I was just postponing the inevitable fact that my gender identity would have to be dealt with, yet it would take many more years to build up that type of courage.

Every match I had in the following year resulted in another concussion, some mild and some more serious. I decided in early 2000 that I would retire the Cobra character and go under a mask as a Mexican high-flyer called "Extremo Loco". It was a bit of a change to wrestle under a face mask but I wanted to make the character a mystery and was so inspired by the Mexican Lucha Libre style that I wanted to be one. I had some decent matches this time against Steve Frost, Jimmy Mustang and Bradman and it concluded with a semi-main event at the NWA Anniversary show in June against Chucky in a steel cage. The match won the Australian Match of the Year for 2000 but it was pretty ordinary in my opinion. The bars of the cage were brutal on my body and I was bruised for weeks afterwards. The finish had Chucky pinning me by giving me a powerbomb off the top turnbuckle onto a table covered in thumbtacks. I got an infection in my elbow from a tack getting lodged so deep it took a pair of pliers to remove it.

Again around August of that year, I was invited to perform at the annual AWF "Psychotic Slam" event but only for the Melbourne show as the opening match against Jimmy Mustang. I arrived at LaTrobe University for the event which also featured 2-Cold Scorpio, Psychosis, Blitzkrieg, Jason Helton, TNT, Psycho Kid Thunder, Lobo, Chucky and Con Iakavidis. I had begun drinking again and I showed up before the show after downing half a bottle of Port. It would prove to be a huge error as I went for my signature move in my match against Jimmy Mustang where I dived through the ropes onto my opponent on the outside of the ring. The last time I performed it as Cobra I broke my right hand but, this time as Extremo Loco, it would be my nose. I was meant to win the match but as soon as I smashed my face onto the hardwood floor I knew I was in serious trouble. I had my mask on and I instantly felt a warm sensation all over as blood began to pour out of my nose. It was a serious break and my nose was sideways on my face. I told Jimmy to just pin me as I couldn't continue. I had to be carried out of the ring by the referee.

Off to the Austin hospital it was, and I knew I was pretty much done as a performer. Over the next couple of years I worked at the shows doing sound and even ended up working at Crown Casino for "All-Star Wrestling" as the sound and lighting director. I had a few more matches in a promotion called PCW (Professional Championship Wrestling) based out in Dandenong. It was a great time but my desire and hunger to be great had already vanished. At this time Lobo, Spike Steele, Johnny Rave and Mad Dog McCrea were becoming the finest wrestlers in Australia and two of them were about to get national press attention for an upcoming event called "Carnage" in September of 2002.

I remember chatting with Lobo and Mad Dog on the phone during the week prior as they discussed ideas for the match. They were about to create history with one of the most violent matches ever conceived in Australia. The ring ropes were removed and replaced with barbed wire. There were 40,000 thumbtacks on a bucket above the ring and set to be randomly dropped. The two fighters dipped their hands into super glue and their knuckles into a tray of broken glass. I was in the front row upon receiving a complimentary ticket as Mad Dog's guest.

It was one of the most disturbing matches I had ever seen. Similar matches were held regularly in Japan which I had watched on video, but to see it only meters away truly shocked me and I was concerned for my friends. Lobo "juiced" himself so deeply that it poured out of his forehead like a tap of running water. I was worried that he might lose consciousness from the loss of blood or even die. The crowd was stunned and some people were in shock. To be fair though, the audience was warned on multiple occasions that this would be extremely graphic. I honestly cannot put into words how far these two guys took it: to the next level and beyond. I was blown away and in disbelief at the amount of true pain they must have been in.

The media response the following week was extremely negative. It was a feature story on radio and television with interviews by Bulldog O'Reily and Gene Gatto. I think the main problem and why they spoke out was because PCW was an off-shoot of the traditional wrestling industry in Australia. Traditionally wrestlers and promoters had to go through a vetting system to see how badly they wanted to be involved and most failed. Ken Rock, owner of PCW, just created his own company without consulting with the decades-long veterans who controlled the industry. PCW had become hated by all other promotions but I saw the future in their athletes. They truly had become world-class performers and it was a shame that this match would cause them to close their doors for several years.

I knew it was time to move on. I had done too much permanent damage to my brain and body and any bump would now cause me a concussion. It was time to find another distraction that would help me block out the inevitable gender dysphoria issues that were building up and becoming stronger as each year passed.

Chucky powerbombing me on the hardwood pub floor

Moonsault off a couch

Ricky Diamond suplexing me through a table off the top

Chucky throwing me over a balcony

Cage match at the Epping Centre

Steve Frost, Tash, Extreme Dream Chucky, Adrian Manera, Stevie Cool, Mel, JT Robinson, Rohan, TNT Havok, Jag, Cobra, Man in Black, Adam Kember

Wrestlerage crew on tour in Adelaide

Pics courtesy of Adam Kember

CHAPTER 5

MAGIC

I remember watching a movie on television around mid-2001. It was a classic starring Tony Curtis as Harry Houdini. It fascinated me and I began the slow and frustrating entry into the world of sleight-of-hand magic. My first trick was something my Dad showed me as he was trying to incorporate little tricks into his night-time job working as a special event organizer and MC for several venues. It took a good few weeks of daily practice to be able to make that silk handkerchief vanish and reappear.

My next tricks were the standard Cups and Balls and some rubber band illusions. I found a local magic shop in Camberwell called "Abracadabra" run by David Brown and Laurie Kelly. You had to go down to the lower basement to find it and I thought that was the coolest shop ever. I dare say that I would spend a fair bit of money and time there over the next couple of years. Laurie was a legend in the worldwide magic scene and was now semi-retired and his guidance truly made me excel much more quickly than teaching myself.

I began obsessing over all forms of magic and dreamed of one day doing big illusions like David Copperfield. I eventually wrote a research paper called "The Secrets of David Copperfield, For Magicians Only" and had it for sale at that very shop. Some of my favorite magicians were Penn and Teller, Bill Malone, David Blaine, Mike Ammar, Jay Sankey, Houdini and mentalists like Uri Geller and Guy Bavli. I even ended up inventing a few tricks, one of which I licensed to Brad Christian at "Ellusionist" in the United States for a couple of years: A mentalism effect called the "Ultimate Watch Stop" where you borrow someone's analog watch, wave your hand over it and it stops ticking. The watch is shown around for the spectator to study, then the magician waves their hand back over the watch to restart the ticking. There is nothing up the sleeve and it can be done naked to prove there are no dodgy gimmicks involved. I wouldn't recommend that, but it was an expression used in the description.

After I felt I was confident enough I would do free weekly magic shows at retirement villages and I loved entertaining there, while also doing stall-type acts at various venues as my alter-ego "Harry Masters". Tricks like the "Three Shell Game" and various card tricks would have patrons in awe and I felt so proud of myself for excelling in such a hard art form.

I met Australia's premier magician Tim Ellis at Coopers Hotel in the city for the monthly magicians networking event called "Coopers Magic Nights". I had seen him on a video doing "Runaround Sue" which was an incredible re-imaginative version of the old cups and balls trick. I videotaped my version of his trick and gave it to him and I was pleasantly surprised to get an e-mail from him praising my work. Another trick that I learned from him was called "Ultimate Blades" where you would swallow five razor blades, a piece of string and regurgitate them attached in even intervals tied together. This was actually a dangerous act to get right, if you messed it up you would probably die on the way to the hospital.

By this time I had several pets for my magic show including four doves, four budgerigars and one mouse. It became a lot of work but I had some decent success in training them all, especially the budgies. To be honest they were my only friends at the time as I was diagnosed with severe depression and anxiety and put on Zoloft, which I ended up on the highest dose possible and still take now. I was also seeing a counsellor regularly for my social anxiety but I never divulged the true issue of my sadness.

Looking back, I started to notice a habit forming of filling my life with whatever I was obsessed with at that particular time to avoid the shame that I thought "coming out" would be. Doing magic distracted me from my inner feelings and I now miss it quite a bit. I don't think I would use animals again, but it would be good to have a card routine instead of the one trick I occasionally do now for friends.

Watching modern magicians on television is interesting because, although they seem to be very good illusionists, they use some camera tricks which was a big no-no when I was studying the art. Criss Angel and Dynamo are notorious for camera tricks, but I must admit they do a great job of it.

David Blaine, who revolutionised the craft, finishes his TV specials with a stunt that is always quite dangerous. Things like being frozen in ice, buried alive, holding his breath underwater for seventeen minutes or starving himself in a plexiglass box for forty-two days are on the verge of a potential death wish. Then how does he top that? Maybe surviving a crucifixion might do it...

I must say though that I think David Copperfield is the best magician to have ever lived in my lifetime. His presentation skills and charisma are a bit old-school, but he still has enough respect for the art form to not use cameras in any other way other than to film his show.

Linking Rings

The stars of the show

Milkshake Cups & Balls

RETURN TO MUSIC

Eventually my magic desire faded, just like everything preceding it and I found myself seriously thinking about returning to music so I dusted off the guitar and went full-on back into practicing many hours a day and in turn, it would develop eventually into tendinitis and carpal tunnel issues. I had pushed it way too hard and too quickly in anticipation of my audition to try out for the Advanced Diploma of Music at Box Hill Institute. I was extremely disappointed to find out a few weeks later that my application was unsuccessful. I was a fairly decent guitarist and yet even Darren Jones, a future classmate and brilliant musician, got rejected as well. But as fate would have it we finally got accepted in mid-January of 2004 after a couple of spots became available.

I was continually getting counselling for my social anxiety and I have no real answer as to why I would want to go back to study in a performing arts environment. I think subconsciously I wanted to face the beast that has destroyed my self-confidence, but it would be years until I would finally begin to get there. There were quite a few young and very talented people in my class including Jaimi Faulker who would later go on to be a huge international success in Europe. He was a killer blues guitarist and a remarkable singer, just like Darren. I felt inferior to any of the guitarists training there. Music came very easy to me as far as writing and theory, but guitar playing forced me to work ten times harder than anyone else and the results seemed that of an average player.

The old music building at BHI

An awesome opportunity came up around my first year of study, it was a lesson with a master virtuoso. As a kid, I first saw guitarist Brett Garsed on the John Farnham television special "Whispering Jack in Concert". I was floored that the guitar could be played like that. It seemed he had mixed the 80s metal guitar/Van Halen style with Allan Holdsworth but with his unique re-inventing of the hybrid. I met him at a guitar clinic at "Soundworks" in Ringwood and asked if he did lessons. I was so privileged and fortunate that he gave me his e-mail and a month or so later I had a two-hour private lesson at his home in Sydenham. He is such a humble genius and willing to help any guitarist by passing along his years of advice. I walked away feeling very honoured and excited to start working through his suggestions.

The lecturers at Box Hill Institute of Music were incredible virtuosos. Mario Lattuada and Rob Bratetich were my guitar teachers and my mouth would drop in awe at their incredible knowledge and musicianship. Plus they were also great guys full of humour and always willing to spend extra time out of class explaining things. Other remarkable teachers included Adam Quaife, an enormously talented sound engineer and producer, Neil Kennedy the aural ear training genius and bassist Ashley Smith. My end-of-semester recital had some great musicians in the small audience including Jaimi, who was a stand-out star amongst the entire student body. He left me a secret message on my tape recorder just before my audition as I was recording it, thanking me for all the great times and good memories.

A few months after finishing my course a really unfortunate and horrible event took place with my former classmate Darren Jones. He was an amazing guitarist and we had become very good friends over the two years of studying at Box Hill Institute. He had become a father the previous year and it was the proudest achievement in his life. A week before the untimely incident my housemate Michelle Welsh and I went to see him play in his band called "Love Jones" at the "Aztec Bar" in Belgrave. I hadn't seen him since graduating and he was thrilled another guitarist came to cheer him on. Getting home from Belgrave after midnight meant repeated calls to hire a taxi and the hours ticked on by until around four in the morning. He waited outside the closed venue with us and told us how great his life was going. He had just been accepted to the Victorian College of the Arts and there was a sparkle in his eyes.

On Thursday, February 26th of 2006, he was traveling on the Belgrave line train from the city to return home. He was randomly stabbed with a huge hunting knife by an unknown stranger, Corey Acuna, who was high on drugs. He bled out on the platform at Box Hill train station and in less than a minute he passed away. I was upstairs near the food court and suddenly police and the media were everywhere. I had a bad feeling, an instinct in my soul that subconsciously told me someone I knew was in big trouble.

Later that evening a housemate called to inform me it was indeed someone I knew. It crushed me and it honestly took me many months to come to terms with the loss and the senselessness of it all. At the graduation ceremony, his name was called out alphabetically after mine and his parents joined the class on stage in his absence. I have never seen two people more broken and looking like life had been sucked from their faces. It was a very sad evening.

Darren Jones with his son Jett

I was still having moderate to severe pain in my wrist and it would eventually force me to abandon performance in pursuit of composing and songwriting at around mid-2006. I wouldn't be able to seriously practice guitar for well over five more years. I began drinking again, firstly once or twice a week, and eventually, it became almost every day. I was sharing a house in Mitcham that had become a "drinking house" and to be honest I have never liked the taste of any alcohol. I drink to bury the pain of being me and for absolutely no other reason. I had started to swap from drinking spirits and wine to beer, a decision that would see me gain a lot of weight and bloat up my face.

I had become a close friend of the pastor at Mitcham Baptist Church, Matt Glover, after Darren's passing. He came over one night about a week after the horrible incident to our house to check up on how we were all going. That was also the night that I confided in him privately about my identity issues and his response blew my mind: "If you are trying to get rid of me, you will have to do better than that!". He was such a caring man, only a year older than myself and we have remained close lifelong friends ever since, even through our own personal visits to hell and back. A genius of a man, just like his sons, with integrity and unselfishness second to none.

Now that I was a regular visitor and member of Mitcham Baptist Church, every Thursday I would go to a house in Nunawading for a "small group" meeting led by an older couple Bert and Jean Eadon where we studied the Bible intensely with other MBC members. The reason I embraced religion again was because a few of my new friends from Box Hill Institute the previous year were Christians including my housemate, Michelle.

I started to play guitar, albeit very lightly due to my ongoing wrist pain issues, at Church a few months later as part of the Music Worship Team and I felt that Darren had passed along a small part of his talent to me. I didn't care about the guitar now that I was a composer and I think that release of not caring took my guitar-playing skills and aural skills to a new dimension. I could now play melodies I was hearing in my head, something I wasn't able to do prior.

As I continued to play guitar in the Church Worship Team I got to play a few times with fellow church attendee Andrew Kitchen from the band "Antiskeptic". He was the only one around my standard professionally and was signed to a record label so we would tear it up on stage, sometimes I would even switch it up and play bass guitar. I got to do a show one night with a younger guy called Jimmy Rietmeyer and to be honest, he was out of his league. It was a total disaster. He would eventually become a fantastic band leader many years later and we got along very well and arranged to hang out at the church sometime during the week as he was a keen aspiring songwriter.

I have never felt comfortable having a songwriting partner but have often contributed parts to many other writing sessions at Box Hill Institute. I even get royalty cheques from some song I helped write that went top ten in Italy. I asked APRA (performing rights company in Australia) if they had made a mistake but they assured me no and I was indeed a fully credited co-songwriter of that hit which I have no memory of contributing to. It must have been some time when I sat around jamming and they included me for some idea I must have added, but considered just a throw-away.

Our first of several great catchy songs was "Hey God". I wrote the majority of the music and we both collaborated on the lyrics. We recorded it at my home mini-studio and his girlfriend Sarah added some great harmonies. We became all super close friends over the next year and formed a Christian rock band called "This Way Up". Eventually, my problems arising from my undiagnosed borderline personality put an end to our friendship forever. At the annual dinner for the performing arts department, I got so drunk that I couldn't remember yelling at Jimmy. It was the beginning of the end. I was a really terrible Christian.

Just before that time, I was invited to see a band called "Selah-phonic" it it was a gig with a big multimedia screen on the side with videos syncing up to the music and it broke me down. The way the singer discussed his struggles with abuse and depression and his redemption through God affected me on a profound level. I remember sitting there in tears while friends comforted me. I wanted to be able to move people in such a spiritual way.

Thanks to being the Dux of my class while completing my Advanced Diploma in Music, I was entered into the second year of the Bachelor of Music degree but was forced to swap from a performance major to composition, thanks to my carpel tunnel flaring up to the point that I couldn't play for more than ten minutes at a time. Composition is a general term that can cover actual orchestral or instrument compositions to songwriting and creating soundtrack music for films. I had amazing lecturers guiding me through all these facets including Mark Buys, George Papanicolau, Lachlan Wilson, Peter Hurley, Jonathan Dimond, Brett Rosenberg and Peter Farnan from "Boom Crash Opera".

My favorite teacher, who would later become a great personal friend, was Mark Buys. He was a former Box Hill Institute graduate and had completed his Masters degree at the College of the Arts. He taught everything related to writing music for the screen and I was fortunate enough to work as his assistant on a feature film directed by Michael Adante called "The Line". It starred David Barry, Andy McPhee and Peter Phelps and centred around the underworld of Melbourne's gangland killings. It came at an unfortunate time because the "Underbelly" television series was only a few months from being released and it ended up being the phenomenon that it was. Mark never got paid for that job of being the film's composer and neither was I but it was a great learning experience. He left about six months later to live in Los Angeles and work with composer Christopher Young and would remain there for several years building up his portfolio of films and television music.

The next couple of years became an obsession for me as I learned from the best and realised the craft of composition takes much more time than instinctually writing a pop song once a tune pops into your head. I explored all types of composing from solo piano pieces, string quartets, jazz big band and full orchestrations to becoming one of the top film score students at the Institute. After I worked for Mark my learning curve excelled far beyond any other student in all year levels and for that I am eternally grateful to Mark for throwing me in the deep end. Every year during the Christmas and January break I would do a research paper just for my own personal knowledge and satisfaction. The two big ones were titled "An Introduction to Middle East & Arabic Music" and an "Introduction to Balinese Gamelan". I don't know why I barely showed them to anyone but it was just my way of learning about world/ethnic music which has always intrigued me.

Somewhere around this time, The Beach Boys were touring Australia and I heard that they would be getting interviewed on radio station 3AW by Denis Walter. On the off-chance I might get some exposure I sent him a remake of a Beach Boys song "Dance, Dance, Dance" and to my surprise he played it just at the start of the interview, also naming me and saying I did all of the five-part vocal harmony parts. I was blown away to get a few minutes on the radio and Denis e-mailed me back saying it was great. Twenty-five or so years of studying their music and to have such an accomplished musician play my recreation made me feel very proud of myself. The harmony study would play a major part in a future band where I would become the musical director and write all the band's vocal parts.

In February of 2008, I started the final year of my Bachelor degree at Box Hill Institute and one of my subjects was called "Negotiated Project" where you chat with the lecturer about something you would like to do in the following semester. My answer had been something on my mind for over a decade. An album that told my life story similar to "The Wall" by Pink Floyd. A journey into the darkest depths of mental health and a redemption that would follow. That album would be my magnum opus...

This entire one-hour-long autobiographical concept album "The Void", was written in just over two months while also studying full-time. I would come home from university and work on it until I fell asleep around midnight. My vocal skills for singing lead were a bit limited so I brought in some friends as guest vocalists including Owen Prout, Sharon McRae and Holly Tampling. My Dad helped me with a fair bit of the post-production and I did the final tweaks and mastering before designing an album cover and submitting the final product in early May.

Psychologically it messed me up getting so deeply into my life story, much like this book, and I was an absolute emotional wreck upon finishing it. To meditate every day about so much pain and find a way of turning it into words and music was an exhausting endeavor but I look back at it with extreme pride, I just wish there were no religious aspects to the message anymore because I left religion a year or so after completing the album. "The Void" was awarded "Oustanding Achievement" by the faculty at Box Hill Institute and was also distributed digitally worldwide in 2017 by record label DJD Global Music Ltd, where it was the highest played and watched music video in their catalog. I think the album is best described through its lyrics...

Pics from my original writing sessions

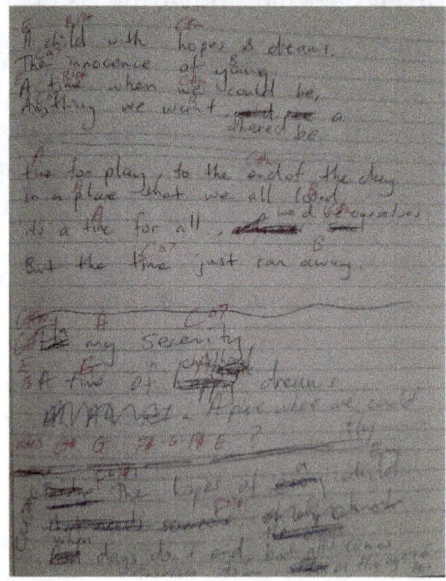

Bully

Riff
He walks across the schoolyard as
a teacher walks on by.
She grabs him by the neck and
he just wonders why?
"you're a bad boy now, I
told you not to lie"
So I will scar you now, for
the rest of your life

Pre CH As he begins to cry
Class is laughing at me
I hope you learned this time
she says to me

Chorus
Abuse Me now & take my
soul away from me.
Refuse my cries to let me go,
as you hold me down...
          Who you're abusing me

V2) The endless torment in my
    dreams, defeat is mine
    And self destruction it does
    seem,   a worthy kind

Pre CH2) What do I do, where can I go
         My life is not easy
         I remember, in my

My Dad's mixing notes

All my demos & ideas from age 12 onwards

BEYOND TRANS

Album cover and credits

The Void is a project that has been on mind for over ten years. As an autobiographical concept album it will hopefully take you, the listener, on a journey through my life and in turn perhaps you can relate to some of my experiences. Life is hard a lot of the time and my intention in creating this is to let you know that there is a way out of our own void. I hope and pray that you will be touched somehow by this project and I feel truly blessed to be able to share my proudest piece of work with you...*Ash*

1. WELCOME TO THE WORLD
Lead Vocal - Holly Tampling
Backing Vocals - Mike Ford (bass vocal) &
Ashley Jackson (all others)
Instruments: Ashley Jackson

2. A PLACE WHERE WE COULD FLY
Lead Vocal - Holly Tampling
Backing Vocals - Ashley Jackson
Instruments: Ashley Jackson

3. TUMBLE DOWN
Lead Vocal - Ashley Jackson & Sharon McRae
Backing Vocals - Ashley Jackson
Instruments: Ashley Jackson

4. ABUSE ME
Lead Vocal - Owen Prout
Guitars - Ashley Jackson

5. YOUNG & LEARNING
Lead Vocal - Ashley Jackson & Sharon McRae
Backing Vocals - Ashley Jackson & Sharon McRae
Instruments: Ashley Jackson

6. INTO THE VOID
Instruments: Ashley Jackson

7. LONELY
Lead & Backing Vocals - Ashley Jackson
Instruments: Ashley Jackson
Saxophone - Lachlan Wilson

8. THE SCREAMING
Instruments: Ashley Jackson

9. CAN YOU HEAR ME?
Vocals & Instruments: Ashley Jackson

10. ON MY OWN (part 1)
Vocals & Instruments: Ashley Jackson

11. I'M SORRY
Lead Vocal - Owen Prout & Sharon McRae
Instruments: Ashley Jackson

12. OUT OF THE VOID
Instruments: Ashley Jackson

13. ON MY OWN (part 2)
Vocals & Instruments: Ashley Jackson

14. YOUR LOVE
Lead Vocal - Sharon McRae
Instruments: Ashley Jackson

15. FREE
Lead Vocal - Holly Tampling & Ashley Jackson
Instruments: Ashley Jackson

ALBUM DIALOGUE by Sharon McRae, Owen Prout,
Holly Tampling, Mike Ford & Ashley Jackson
Recorded between May & June 2008

PRODUCED BY ASHLEY JACKSON

Welcome to the World

Hide away 'til the morning meets the sun
Find a way to hope and you'll run
Fly away 'til the sun meets the sea
Everybody's welcome, welcome to the world with me

A Place Where We Could Fly

A child with hopes and dreams
The innocence of young
A time when we could be anything we want
There'd be a time for play to the end of the day
In a place that we all loved
It's a time for all, we'd be ourselves
But the time just ran away
For my serenity
A time of childhood dreams
A place where we could fly

The wonder in all our hearts
The happiness within
My world seemed bigger then
Waiting for some new hope of fitting in with all my friends
But the smile starts to undone
And happy times I thought were mine
Would soon cause me to run

The hopes of a child
When days don't end
But all comes crashing down
At the age of ten...

Tumble Down

He walks across the schoolyard as a teacher walks on by
She grabs him by the neck and he is asking why?
"You've been a bad boy now, I told you not to lie
So I will scar you now for the rest of your life"
As he begins to cry
Class is laughing at me
"I hope you learned this time"
she says to me

She says "It's not OK
And you'll stay like that 'til the end of the day
Hey look!" They laugh at me
And the tears start rolling and tumble down

A year or two has passed and now I'm on my way
to a high school that made me dread all days
Coz after classes stopped a bus would save my life
For if it didn't come then the bashings showed the signs
Of a child already broken
And the times I'd eat the dirt, the mud
The times they spat on me

They say "It's not OK to fight back now
Or we will change your life today"
I pray they'll go away
As the tears start rolling and tumble down

Abuse Me

I've been living in a hole so deep and wide
Another day of drinking to numb my mind
I remember when I was younger
The older kids hurt me
And the nightmares of that story
Take me back and starts again

Abuse me now and take my soul away from me
Refuse my cries to let me go as you hold me down
When you're abusing me

The endless torment in my dreams, defeat is mine
And self destruction it does seem a worthy kind
What do I do? Where do I go?
My line is not that easy
I remember in my nightmares
It takes me back and starts again

Abuse me now and take my soul away from me
Refuse my cries to let me go as you hold me down
When you're abusing me

Young & Learning

I've just discovered love and it's beautiful to say
You're my true love 'til the end of every day
But there's a frightened thought within my mind
That I might lose the love I've searched hard to find
I'm young and I'm still learning and I've found my true peace
It's in your voice and your warmth that will never cease

I need your love to help me through
To find my way, to find the truth
My feelings are I need you
Love of my life

I never know why it's just the way I feel
Within you near me my pain is so unreal
But there's a frightened thought within my mind
That I might lose the love I've searched hard to find
I'm young and I'm still learning and I've found my true peace
It's in your voice and your warmth that will never cease

I need your love to help me through
The greatest friend I have in you

If we don't find an answer today on this road so long
Then it's the end of this love that's so strong
I'm young and I'm still learning and I've found my true peace
It's in your voice and your warmth that will never cease

Lonely

Feeling left out most of the time
Lonely feelings deep inside
I need you to comfort me all of my life
Nowhere to turn, no place to hide

Love is the one word I can't deny
Is this the way? Nowhere in life
Wasting my time, drinking my life away
When all I need is you right now

When you call for help
It seems there's nothing left and why
I keep calling for you
I never wanna have to say goodbye

Feeling so empty, lost in life
Depressed in a state near suicide
If I can't be with you I wanna die

Time brings healing for I can't make it alone
It's time I was leaving, pick up my bags and run
Time brings healing for I can't make it alone
Time to stop breathing
Putting my head to a gun

On My Own

Feeling sad it's hard to see what you've really done to me
And every day I wonder why my lonely heart will not subside

I'm taking the time coz that is what I'm needing
I'm living out here all on my own

Hurt is nothing new to me, What is my reality?
And they don't know the way I feel, The pain in my heart needs to heal

I'm taking the time coz that is what I'm needing
I'm living out here all on my own
I'm living a lie coz time it just won't heal me
I'm living out here all on my own

Then someone rescued me while others let me go
Helping me to be and helping me to grow

Now I've found my way I see
That they really care for me

I'm taking the time coz that is what I've needed
I'm living out here, I'm not alone
I'm learning to fly
To share my own true feelings
I live without fear out on my own
Out here on my own
Out here I'm not alone

I'm Sorry

Silence greets the morning sun
Cast away a loaded gun
But in the wake of ocean
Lies a timely notion

Try to keep your mind apart
But when you're lost where do you start?
Signs of new direction
Fight with inspiration

I'm sorry I was bad
My mind was going mad
And how can I forgive myself?
How can I move on?
When all my life has gone
I miss you tonight... Where is the light?

Who am I and who are you?
Have you found your lifetime truth?
Why am I the bad guy?
Accept the fate of my life?

There must be more to life
I've searched but I can't find
The love I need... or inner peace of mind
I'm sorry

Your Love

Here in my heart it tears me apart
I need a new beginning
Trampled upon, Do I belong?
Do I have a meaning?
Although I've turned my back
To all of your teachings
Every time I cry your name
You'll never leave me

I need your love
I need to know your healing
And Why? Why do you just forgive me?
I know coz no one loves me like you do

I need your help coz I'm hanging on but barely
Answer my call, it might seem small
But I believe in you
Although I've turned my back
The times I've been screaming
Every time I cry your name
You'll never leave me

As I crawl under my blankets and cry
Geez! please help me and make me alive

Although I've lived in pain
The past is behind me
Every day's a new day
With you here beside me

I need your love
need to know your teachings
And I thank you for your healing
And please just know that I love you
That I love you

DRUM SEQUENCING, KEYBOARDS, GUITARS & BASS
by Ash Jackson
ALTO SAXOPHONE by Lachlan Wilson
ALBUM MIXED BY ASH & BILL JACKSON
PRODUCED BY ASH JACKSON

CHAPTER 7

LIFE CONFUSION

While continuing my further studies I started experimenting with my gender expression by painting my nails, wearing mascara, jewelry and ladies' jeans with sandals or ballet flats. I got a few looks but it slowly built up my confidence to carry an androgynous handbag and style my hair with a high ponytail. I wanted to wear a dress to the end-of-year Institute ball and graduation, but I chickened out and eventually fell out or lost touch with most of my classmates. Even back then in 2008 being gay was not accepted and most people I knew often joked about it, so being transgender wasn't even on anyone's radar as anything but disgusting. We all have struggles of course but mine was questioning my very existence.

I had come out as trans to my Mum years before but it was now time to tell the rest of my family and telling my Dad was the hardest part. Overall my family has been accepting which I am grateful for because many others lose their family when they reveal their lifelong secret. Most of my family still call me "he" and it feels like a punch in the guts but I imagine it must be hard for them.

Coming out to my church was not so warm and I was ostracised and asked to leave the Music Worship Team which showed me a lot about religion and in particular Mitcham Baptist Church. I remained in contact with a few of them including Matt Glover, who had left Mitcham Baptist Church for a senior position at Lilydale Baptist Church. He was fired from his position in Lilydale after about two years upon revealing his well-researched beliefs that the LGBT community was doing nothing wrong and that all Christians should accept them. I remember the hour-long phone calls with him as he faced an uncertain future and I truly felt so disgusted at the cowardice displayed by the church.

My faith began to fade over that time to the point that I hated all religions and was left as an atheist. During my last visit to the church I was in transition and showed up in a dress but was appalled when the senior pastor got everyone to stand up and pray that the plebiscite election for the recognition of gay marriage in Australia would not go through. I was so disgusted and I knew they were never going to change, so I walked out and have never returned since.

The night I left I went to hail a taxi and each time a cab driver asked where I was going. They obviously realised I was transgender and drove off. The last car opened its window on the passenger's side and I put my upper body in leaning while I asked if I could go a few kilometres to my home. He refused and took off while I was still leaning into the window and I was forced to raise my legs as he took me for the ride of my life. I begged him to stop and he told me to let go. I finally did at the beginning of the Eastern Freeway ramp where I rolled into a traffic barrier at around

80 kilometres an hour. I was relieved to be alive and that nothing was broken but my ankle was bleeding profusely and I crawled home for over a kilometre, which seemed like it took hours. Not a single car pulled up to help me. I developed a bone infection on my left ankle that took months to finally heal. To my knowledge that taxi driver was never charged with anything and I have been nervous about catching taxis ever since.

I would occasionally go to a wrestling show to visit my friends including Chucky, Ricky Diamond, Bulldog, Mad Dog and the legend himself George Julio. Another friend that I was starting to follow quite closely was Matthew Muir, known as "Jungle Cat". When I was at my peak he was just starting and he certainly had "the look". He was ripped with muscles and went under a mask as a type of bodyguard for the bad guy manager Lord James Earl (Jim Demirov who was then also under a mask). He had been involved in matches here and there around 1999 and 2000, but when I saw him wrestling again around 2009 onwards, I was majorly impressed.

He was still respectful enough to honour the old-school way of improvisation with a few "spots" during his matches which impressed me greatly. Some wrestlers had gone down the way of planning their entire match, which ended up looking like a beautifully choreographed ballet, but Matt made it seem much more real. He had truly paid his dues and was now one of the top athletes in the industry down under. He had now removed the Jungle Cat mask which I thought was a clever move, but my gosh, his wrestling and in-ring character were easily worthy of a full-time career abroad. I would walk away from a show thinking he was the clear standout by far, even surpassing the more experienced, yet somewhat newer veterans like Ricky Diamond and Chucky.

I ended up having a falling out with Chucky when he borrowed about fifty of my VHS wrestling videos from the shows I had filmed, I tried to get them back but all he did was file a fraudulent intervention order claiming I was harassing him. It was honestly nothing more than him being upset because I started a website called "Aussie Wrestling Downloads" to sell digital versions of the shows I had filmed and owned the copyright to. He didn't like this because certain videos portrayed him in a bad light and I refused to remove them. He was always notorious for filing court orders against anyone portraying him in any type of not-so-flattering way.

I went to Sunshine Magistrates Court to fight the order but after a five-hour wait and three hours of driving through peak-hour traffic, I just couldn't be bothered ever returning to that shit-hole of an area again upon a proposed adjournment. Chucky didn't look healthy at all, his stomach made him look like he was "expecting" and he was a shell of the person I was once good friends with. I think that deep down he wasn't able to cope knowing that I was transgender and this was his way of never letting that part of me into his life. He had done this to multiple other people that he felt offended by. Making up some crap for a court order full well knowing there are no consequences for lying on an intervention order application. I agreed without any admission of guilt to the order, as long as I could still run my website but only post his matches that I was involved in. I thought that was a reasonable outcome and I was happy not to return to that area again. I still want my tapes back Chucky. I own the physical VHS cassettes and the intellectual property too as it was filmed on my camera... Jackass!

The following year I got accepted to the University of Melbourne for post-graduate study. It was a great learning experience to study with so many talented geniuses such as Dr Katy Abbot, Dr Andrian Pertout and Dr Stuart Greenbaum. It taught me a lot about perfection and thinking way outside the box when composing, plus making the most out of a simple idea. I never finished the course which I do regret but my folio of compositions, which took hundreds of hours to complete, made me quite proud with a Distinction grade.

Brad, Dad, Mum & me

Fran & Brad on their Wedding day

I love my parents

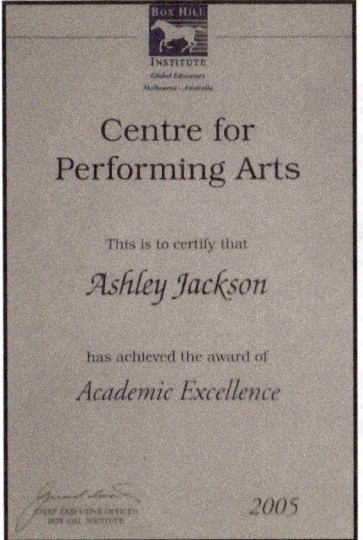
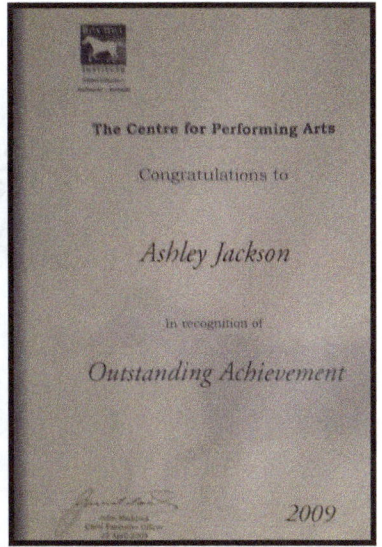

My graduation dress that I didn't wear

OZ FISH TV

As I got closer to my fortieth year of life I started to seek out activities that felt okay to be in solitude with myself and a bit more calming. I started enjoying learning to cook and as always I would obsess over a recipe with a lot of research until I discovered something that worked. I also began an interest in fishing which had not been something I had done since my childhood and teenage years while on holidays at Sorrento or Lake Eildon. My brother Brad told me he often went out on a friend's boat and caught Snapper and Gummy sharks. I bought a highly inappropriate fishing rod from Compleat Angler in Box Hill and began my new journey learning how to catch and eventually cook fish that I would catch like Flathead, Bream, Snapper, Whiting and Calamari.

I became quite good at catching Calamari in Port Phillip Bay, usually from a pier such as Mornington, Rye or Portsea using a prawn-shaped lure more commonly known as a "squid jig". I started going out on the occasional fishing charter with skipper

Matt Cini that winter and he taught me the fine art of catching King George Whiting. I started to wonder how the average person could afford to successfully go fishing if they had no boat and had an idea to someday create a DVD or TV show showing accessible and affordable fishing for the everyday angler.

While at Mornington Pier I discovered a charter run by skipper Stuart Maconachie and his wife Sandra. It was here I became friends with a local fishing identity named Glenn Cooper. He was about fifteen years older than me and would either be on the pier daily or out on the boat. We discussed how some of the television fishing programs were extremely unrealistic and nothing that any average person could ever afford. I thought to myself that I may have a guy here who is charismatic enough to host a show like the one I was thinking about maybe pursuing. This of course was all about distracting my mind from the inevitable transgender issue that would lie beneath the surface and deep down I knew it would hit me again as it had so many other times and always stronger than the last.

I had been playing around with names for my show. I ended up settling on "My Fish TV" for about a week before changing it to "Aus Fish TV". I was mucking around with the "IMPACT" font on Photoshop with the word FISH large and in the middle, surrounded by AUS and TV but it didn't look aesthetically balanced so I changed it to OZ and slept on the idea overnight. Then as I turned on my computer the next day and opened Photoshop... OZ FISH TV was born and I told Glenn about the name and he liked it.

I used my father's Sony Handycam and we got to filming at Mornington Pier in June and July of 2013. Glenn's stage name was now "Guru Glenn" as I suggested and at around the same time he was doing a weekly fishing report on local radio, so there was a small buzz in the community thanks to his comments about a new realistic fishing show he was a part of. I had never done any serious video editing and like usual I threw myself in the deep end with what would turn out to be hundreds and eventually thousands of hours learning the craft. The first edits of "Oz Fish TV" were that of Glenn catching a Snapper from the pier and it was okay footage, but I felt an extra co-host would make it more accessible.

I met Chris Monnier on a fishing charter and he had become a regular down at the pier while I was filming. One day in August I asked if he wanted to stand next to Glenn and just react with some colour commentary. The footage was great as Chris is quite a charismatic and humourous guy so a light bulb moment entered my thoughts: Glenn and Chris to host the show with myself doing everything else as the show's creator and producer.

I had an idea for some cool rock guitar music for the show's soundtrack so I reached out to Brett Garsed again and asked permission to use his solo music which he gladly agreed to. The show's theme was now an edited version of his catchy instrumental "Fu'd Fight" and we began filming a few times a week at Mornington Pier and Glenn's home in Frankston.

In September we arranged for a trip to Bemm River in East Gippsland with another local nicknamed Fast Eddie. All four of us would be spending about a week there filming and we rented a two-story house right next to the hotel and a couple of hundred meters from the water. But family life was about to throw a huge curveball when my sister-in-law's brother Julian went missing from his home in Tasmania. He had a lot of personal issues and also drank alcohol to a huge extent just like me. About a week after he went missing he was found in a car and had taken his own life with carbon monoxide poisoning. He was only thirty years old and my family went down to Tasmania for the funeral.

It was a sad time with the funeral hall was packed. There were comments all day about how they wished Julian could see how many people loved him. My only problem with that was that most of them had abandoned him during his time of need. He had tried to reconnect with some of them but to no avail and yet there they were proclaiming how much of a great friend they were to him. I had enormous respect for Julian and we would occasionally chat online mostly about music as he was a bass guitarist. My thought on suicide has always been that if you feel that unhappy then you have every right to end your existence, because you can't live for someone else if you hate your own life.

I could not wait to get back home and couldn't wait to get away from daily life and take some time out on a fishing/filming trip to Bemm River the following day. Eddie and Glenn drove Eddie's car on the long journey while Chris came down a few days later. His wife was pregnant and it seemed to upset him quite a bit as they would argue quite often, which I imagine would be quite understandable, so he was relieved to get away from home life for a few days. Chris had done quite well for himself in the corporate world but had been let go from his high-paying executive role in the egg farming industry due to him calling out others in the organisation for unethical behavior or something very similar.

He lived in a beautiful house in Mornington and was married with two kids. His smart witty humour and charisma always impressed me as to the fact that he was a very accomplished drummer who used to play in some of Melbourne's top cover bands. He also knew of George Kristy who I wrestled with years ago and was also a top drummer, but had also committed suicide not too long ago which brought back fresh memories of Julian.

Our time there at Bemm River was great with a lot of fishing on land and in boats as well as daily visits to the pub, games of pool, a lot of drinking and laughing thanks to Chris and Glenn's ribbing of each other. One night I told Chris about my gender dysphoria and it was a relief to learn of his compassion and serious side to him. Over the next few weeks once we returned to Melbourne I came out to some of the regulars in my new fishing community and it was met with a lot of understanding and questions. I guess I felt comfortable enough to take another gamble and risk the friendships but as it turned out I had nothing to be concerned about, or so I thought.

It was around this time that Glenn, Chris and I made a verbal agreement to be three-way partners in "Oz Fish TV" as I sent my first draft of the pilot TV show to Channel 31 in Melbourne. The feedback was promising but they asked for me to have another go with more host interaction and to study some other fishing shows to see their editing and production styles. We were now in October of 2013 and I had posted a message on a forum asking if anyone knew a reliable fishing spot for an upcoming television show that was land-based but on the other side of the peninsula at Western Port. I received a message from a young guy named Jesse Hommelhoff and he invited me to come down to Warneet pier on the weekend and he guaranteed some Whiting for starters and maybe other species.

It was a great afternoon of fishing and he did indeed provide me with some decent footage of Whiting being caught as well as describing on camera his rig and bait method. I thought to myself that Jesse might make a good addition as a co-host that might appeal to a younger audience so I asked him if he wouldn't mind contributing to the occasional segment of the show, but also letting him know that Glenn and Chris were the main hosts. He mentioned that a friend of his owned a tackle store in Pakenham and had aspirations of starting a fishing show also, so I agreed to let him pass on my information and things seemed to look like I was heading in a positive direction.

The next day I got a message from a guy who ran a tackle shop called "Pak n Tackle" which was based out of Pakenham, hence the business name abbreviation. He sent me a few clips of him doing different knots and rigs as instructional videos and another lightbulb moment happened. An expert on tackle would make a great segment on each episode so I agreed to drive out to his shop and meet with him. He reminded me somewhat of a working-class version of Chris as he had natural charisma and I was impressed that he had a fishing shop. His name was Michael Del Marco but he preferred to be called Mickey Dee and his enthusiasm was infectious. He told me about his idea for a show called "All Roads Lead to Fishing" and I thought it was okay but quite a mouthful. Once he heard "Oz Fish TV" his eyes lit up and he reveled as I described the segments, potential ideas, music, hosts, concepts and my previous interactions with Channel 31.

It was time to take the show to the next level aesthetically and Mick offered to buy us hats and hoodies with my logo on them if he could be a part of the show. We all agreed this would make the show look much more professional so over the next week we all had our apparel and were ready for the next video shoot at Warneet as we had arranged for two boats to hire. As the show's creator and producer, I thought it might be good for Glenn to step aside and for Chris and Mick to test the waters and see if I could get some type of chemistry happening with these two quite charismatic guys. We got some great footage hunting down some squid and I knew all the stars had aligned. We had the beginnings of something special and different from any other fishing program.

At this time I was now fully transitioning again into my womanhood and was presenting more femininely with my new bunch of friends within the Oz Fish and Mornington community. Nothing too over the top, usually just shorts with a girly t-shirt and a pair of sandals with my hair in a ponytail and some light makeup. The estrogen I had been taking for years had kind of plateaued and I was getting monthly sessions of laser therapy on my face to remove hair which hurt like hell.

On our next trip, we went off to Phillip Island as my Aunty had a holiday house down there and the rent was very cheap. We spent a weekend at various locations and had a great time with a hell of a lot of drinking involved. Glenn and his friends fished and filmed at Rhill Pier while Chris, Jesse and Mick filmed at Cowes Pier. The footage was fairly ordinary from Glenn as nothing significant was caught but he did well in front of the camera. The Cowes team got some great catches including a good-sized gummy shark and footage of an eagle stingray which was extraordinary. There was a little in-between segment of Jesse catching and releasing too many flathead to count with a guest named Stephanie Geier that they all met on the pier, which made a nice balance as I began the long process of editing all this content into a 24-minute episode to pitch to channel 31 again in January of 2014.

We did one more trip before Christmas that year and it was aboard "Bay Fish 'n' Trips" charter out of Mornington. Stuart and Sandra had graciously offered to run a twilight charter with all the proceeds from the customers generously donated so that we could get Mick compensated for the hundreds he had spent on our apparel and towards an extra camera. This was to be overall a great night with some excellent footage but also the last time Glenn would be involved with Oz Fish TV.

There had been tension building amongst Glenn, Chris and Mick since the Phillip Island trip. So much so that Glenn was sarcastically calling it now "The Mickey Dee Show" because of his constant enthusiasm for getting footage and the headquarters seemed to spiritually be in Pakenham at Mick's shop. Towards the end of the night Glenn and Chris, who had been jointly stirring each other up for hours, almost went nose-to-nose with Glenn clenching his fist and making a very quick yet subtle gesture that he might strike Chris. It was even accidentally caught on film as well as the aftermath of Mick cooling them off as we docked the boat and gave Stuart and Sandra a big applause for their generosity.

I spent that night at their home in the guest unit out back of their home and tried to analyse what had just happened over several calls from Chris. The tension had been in the air for a while between those two, but this wasn't friends stirring each other for a laugh, this was serious. Now it felt like something was slipping away and I had no control over the outcome. I awoke to a message forwarded from Chris that he was about to send to Glenn and also send along to Mick. I've never been a fan of sending serious conversations over a text message and always thought the person receiving it should at least be awarded the courtesy of being told face-to-face, or at the bare minimum with a phone call.

The message read along the lines of Chris saying to Glenn that he was "unable to work with him on the show anymore and wished Glenn all the best for the future, but it was either Glenn or him". To me, it sounded too sterile and almost like he had done this many times before in the corporate world. It was like a lawyer had looked over it before it was sent, and he wanted the rest of the crew to also send a message underneath agreeing with him and that Glenn had been let go from the partnership. I reluctantly agreed after a call from Chris telling me that I needed to be very assertive on this and that it would help me grow as a person. I can't remember what I wrote as I was crying at the time but I knew the outcome would be the loss of a friend in Glenn, and that his life was so tied up in this show that it would devastate him. I buried my head in my hands as I pressed send, got up, drove back home to Box Hill and turned my phone off like a coward...

CHAPTER 9

OZ FRAUD TV

In January 2014, Chris and Mick thought we needed to replace the footage of Glenn previously shot at Phillip Island, so we all decided to head back to the island and visit the Rhyill Trout Farm with both of them bringing their young daughters. We got treated with such generous hospitality and I got footage of the girls catching their first fish, as well as some lovely scenic shots as we progressed through the facility and had the fish cooked up by the staff. We also filmed an introductory description of the show's mission statement that I thought would make a nice thirty-second "What Oz Fish TV is about" introduction before the actual music video hit introducing the hosts etc.

Now it was time to nail a kick-ass pilot episode to get the tick of approval from channel 31 so I spent days editing a new intro video with highlights from our footage so far and spotlights on the three hosts in Chris, Mick and Jesse. I sent the draft to the others and they were blown away so I put together a basic framework of the three main segments of the proposed pilot show:

Part one was the trout farm experience, part two was the footage from Cowes Pier and part three began with a Mickey Dee segment describing some fishing knots and tackle from his shop, followed by the bigger catches from Cowes Pier.

Mick was so keen to also learn the behind-the-scenes stuff that he sat with me as we went over the final cuts and added little tweaks to make it as perfect as we could. I saw his enthusiasm so I asked if he would like to be my co-producer and he was over the moon. Now it was time to pitch it to channel 31 again but this time I sent Chris and Mick in person with a USB drive of the pilot to pitch, as I knew their charisma would help to get us over the line this time. Chris had also written out a statistical business plan which the program manager was impressed with, showing the target audience and a lot of angling statistics in Australia. I got a call while they headed out of the meeting. "Approved instantly for thirteen episodes to begin airing in March". Wow! It was now time to find some sponsors so we could financially make this work. They would get a banner for a few seconds before the show started, and so far we had Bay Fish 'n' Trips, Rhyll Trout Farm, Pak 'n' Tackle, Gotcha Bait, Black Magic Tackle and Jarvis Walker amongst a few others.

Our next trip was to the Ninety-Mile Beach along the southern-east coast of Victoria, and in particular Golden Beach, to get some surf fishing footage chasing sharks and any other bi-catch. We invited Stephanie along who the guys had met at Cowes Pier, thinking it might be a nice addition to get her on film showing that it wasn't just a "guy thing" but the ladies could fish too and add a different element to the show. It was also nice to have some fellow female company.

The footage turned out great but it was mostly night fishing while we caught about a dozen gummy sharks and other fish. The camping segments were quite humourous and by the end of the weekend, I was impressed enough with Steph to ask her if she wanted to be involved as a guest co-host and she was quite keen. She never drank much but we made up for that by smashing out around five or six slabs of beer over the weekend. We were all drunk on camera and it also helped pass the long hours of waiting for fish.

Jesse rode in my car the way to and from Golden Beach and we had some great conversations. I was starting to like this young man as a close friend and besides that, he was an angling genius. We also met some nice people who were camping next to us called Scott and Kerry. They had an amazing camp set-up with several separate rooms for them and their kids. They would join us at the campfire and on the beach and we exchanged contact details to keep in touch. A week later I was visiting them at their home in Cranbourne for dinner and drinks and felt like I had made some awesome new friends. They and their children 100% accepted my gender transition which gave me a lot of affirmation emotionally and helped me to express my femininity more freely with pride and enjoyment.

About a week before the show was to debut on television we all did an evening filming session at Patterson River to target one of the most elusive species: Mulloway. This location was a somewhat badly kept secret among the fishing community and by exposing it to everyone on television later in the series we copped a lot of backlash and hate from that same community. Mick, Chris and Jesse all caught Mulloway that night, while Steph caught a gigantic Bream which were all safely and respectfully released.

That night Steph and I crashed at Mick's home in Pakenham

and as we layed out exhausted on the couch, I noticed Mick and Steph flirtingly cuddling each other. I knew she thought he was attractive but my concern was raised because Mick was in a serious relationship with his partner Kim and I had recently become good friends with her. This kind of really shocked me and also that Steph knew this fact, was even more shocking. He was stroking her hair and doing light kisses on her head as we all sat and watched television. I was so stunned that I left to drive home even while being as drunk as a skunk.

My mental health though was starting to deteriorate slowly again. My issues with borderline personality disorder were coming to the surface far too often. I would switch off from people and, although I knew I was doing it, I had yet to get any serious professional help on how to manage BPD. Borderline Personality Disorder can only be managed with counseling over a long period while you learn to live in the moment and with an awareness that you have it. For me, it started around the age of eighteen slashing my arms deep enough to bleed but not enough to make a genuine attempt on my life. It would be something that would continue on and off throughout my life and even into the final stages of writing this book. I have scars on my forearms that will be there for life, like a crap tattoo that is a constant reminder of the times when managing BPD falls by the wayside temporarily.

In March 2014 "Oz Fish TV" made its debut on Channel 31 and Mick had arranged an opening night party at "Pak 'n' Tackle" with about fifty guests including all of our sponsors which was now starting to pay off with around $1000+ a week in profit to keep the show progressing and eventually purchase better equipment. Before it aired I took the team aside, did a group hug and told them how much I loved them all. As the ending played and read "Produced by Ash Jackson with Michael Del Marco" I started crying and the crowd gave us a standing ovation as Chris, Jesse, Mick, Steph and myself took a bow with Chris proceeding to do a thank you speech.

Mick, Chris, Myself, Jesse & Steph at Lake Tyers

I was a bit taken aback as the only mention I got was a thank you for the editing. I thought the sixteen-hour days for no money throughout almost eight months deserved more credit. After all, I created the concept, the segments and the graphics and if it wasn't for me the show would never even exist. I felt like I didn't matter and dwelled on it intensely for the next few days until I lost it again with another BPD incident, this time an extremely serious one. Usually, someone will BPD will feel like they have nothing to live for when they say or write suicide notes. It is a true cry for help. So much anxiety, stress and self-loathing has built up over time that all they want is for their loved ones to show them that they are truly loved and not expendable.

As usual, I had been drinking heavily and felt ignored by the Oz Fish team after my depressing chats over the phone and the internet caused them to exclude me from a filming session at Lang Lang. I was very angry and upset that I, the creator of a TV show that put all their faces on the box, was excluded regardless of my depressing attitude. I sat at my computer and sent messages after trying to call but they all went ignored. I later found out many months after that there was talk for a while between Chris and Mick that they didn't really need me anymore and that their skills as hosts were up there with the best. As I would later also find out, they were scared of the image of me being transgender in the fishing television business when we would meet sponsors and executives.

I wrote on my computer in big letters "Goodbye to the world, the pain of my entire life has become unbearable, I hate myself. I'm sorry to my family" and left it on screen as I headed to my car and took off with a decent amount of booze including a bottle of vodka. I turned my phone off as I parked a couple of kilometers away down a side road near Eram Creek where there was a dead end and began drinking and crying. Then I started cutting myself with a razor blade and stayed there for a few hours repeating it all over and over again.

After polishing off the vodka and a bunch of beer I turned my phone back on. I wanted to call my parents as they deserved to hear my voice and not remember my last words as a typed message. My phone messages were going crazy with messages from my parents, Steph, Jesse, Scott, Kerry but nothing from Chris or Mick. There were also a lot of missed calls from a private number which I presumed was the police. I switched it off again as I did not want the police to trace my location by triangulating the signal from my phone. I even removed the battery and decided I would just do it right now as I smashed the empty bottle and grabbed the remainder of the bottle's neck, which was now a shard representing a knife.

I had researched the difference between cutting my wrists the right way or just slicing the main artery in my neck. The most common initial effects are panic and shock. The wrists would be more like going to sleep slowly while the neck would bleed out quickly. There were cons to each method too: The wrists meant more time to panic and change your mind and the neck was choking to death but was over more promptly. I pressed the knife-edged bottle to my neck and started pressing firmly to stupidly gauge the pain level I would have to endure briefly. A trickle of blood began to follow and I wanted to call my mum. She had brought me into this world after nine months of living inside her tummy and she deserved to hear the words "I love you" so I re-booted my phone.

I called the house phone and my dad picked it up. He said, "Ash your mother is hysterical here, please come home mate...please". The thought of my mum never being able to ever be happy for the rest of her life because of me hit me in an instant, and I asked to speak to her. I was bawling my eyes out with the bottle pressed against my neck as I said: "Mum I love you. You brought me into this world and it's now time to leave. The pain is too much and I want your blessing as I leave this world now"...She replied, "Ash I'm sorry for not understanding you are a girl and I don't want you to hurt anymore, I love you".

I instantly hung up I just lost it, I couldn't take any more of the agony in her voice. I threw the bottle out of the window and switched my phone off again. I can't do this to my parents, they will never recover and to do so would be cutting their lives short. I had seen the impact of Julian's suicide on his mother and she was a destroyed and broken person. I drove the car back and parked it down the street facing my parent's house. I cut the lights as I parked and saw several police cars out the front of their home. I knew I would be done for very high-range drunk driving so I decided to stumble the rest of the way as blood slowly dripped from my arms onto the pavement.

Awaiting me was my dad in the driveway and he hugged me but my brain was now too numb and void of emotion. I was in the midst of a nervous breakdown and my brain had switched off. My mum hugged me and I was like a robot, completely null of any emotion. My soul was broken, my heart was hurting and my brain was too traumatized by alcohol and emotion to understand any realm of the slightest form of reality. The rest of the night was a blur. The police asked me questions out of concern but I didn't say anything. Paramedics showed up as well as Scott and Kerry to support my parents. Their eldest daughter also had BPD so I guess their understanding and compassion made them sympathetic to the events of that night. Off to Box Hill Hospital I went in an ambulance to get stitched up and evaluated by the psychiatry department. I had again disappointed a lot of people but I felt relieved to be alive. That was the closest I had ever been to visiting the great unknown.

The fallout from my so-called "attention seeking" according to Chris, was a similar message on my phone to the one he had sent Glenn months earlier. The usual bullshit saying he cannot continue working with me, that I am a very selfish person etc... When I arrived home the next day the only contact I received was Stuart from the Mornington charter boat. We had become quite good friends and he asked if I wanted to come visit him and

Sandra and stay the night at their house while watching the latest episode on the show which featured a segment on their charter plus a commercial that I had created for them. It felt good to have them on my side as I described how I felt about Chris and Mick. He also agreed he had seen their egos skyrocket and called them "a bunch egomaniacs". I liked that analysis as it meant that what I was feeling and observing was also being noticed by others.

The show was somewhat in limbo yet I still had to deliver the rest of the thirteen-episode season to channel 31. Later in the week Mick called and seemed a bit distant towards me but I suggested we go Friday night for a filming session. He was unsure whether Chris would want to be involved but we organised the team for a twilight fish at Half Moon Bay in Blackrock. Jesse saw me and gave me a massive hug while Chris ignored me until I bit the bullet, became the better person, and apologised.

Things slowly seemed a bit better over the next month but I found myself increasingly losing little bits of control as Mick and Jesse started to make attempts at trimming and editing footage which reminded me, standard-wise, of where I was six months earlier. Stephanie and I had developed a strong bond since she joined the crew, partly because we were the only girls and also because she was a Christian and we would talk about religious matters knowing that I used to be a one. I think the qualities of love, acceptance, forgiveness and kindness are all inherently human values. We all want to live in peace and there is no mystical all-knowing God that makes us intrinsically do that, it's in our human nature. We should not fear death and spend our whole life working towards getting into some fanciful afterlife. Our "heaven" is the here and now so make the most of it, even with your demons and all. Easily said but much harder to do!

Over the next few weeks Steph slowly started to become distant, as did everyone associated with the show. I was used to losing friends because of my BPD issues but this felt subtly different. I knew something was up. I was back to drinking every day, sometimes even driving and full well knowing I should not have but my internal self-hatred was rearing its ugly head again. I also felt guilt over how we had treated Glenn and I wanted to at least reach out and make a mends if that was possible.

I sent him a message asking if it was okay to call and he said yes. The call was fairly lengthy and I apologised for following the others in removing him from the team and he forgave me. It felt good to have that off my conscience and good to know that it was alright to say hello if we bumped into each other. I had a tremendous amount of respect for Glenn and still do. He currently runs free fishing days for kids and disadvantaged youth even though he is most likely still struggling financially just to stay afloat. That to me is a far greater achievement than any television show. I knew someday we would do some type of thing together but I had to get back to producing the rest of the season.

Chris was increasingly becoming difficult and was not pulling his weight on contributing time to the show. Mick, Jesse, Steph and I were out every single weekend and every second or third weekday filming. This also meant a lot of driving and a massive lack of sleep. Fifty minutes each way and my days were quickly back to sixteen hours of editing, filming and creating. I even fell asleep along the Monash Freeway one late night while driving and woke up with an adrenaline rush realising I had crossed three lanes of traffic. I had dodged another bullet...

My family life at this time was causing immense stress on my parents, my brother and sister-in-law. My parents had just left for their first overseas holiday upon retiring and I was left at the house all alone, slowly starting to worry about my sanity and ongoing alcoholism. It was one of the worst times of my life that followed and I selfishly ruined my parents long deserved getaway when things came to a head with my involvement on Oz Fish TV. We had an important filming session on a weekend in May and Chris pulled out again to fill in as a drummer in a band. I was happy for him to do the gig but it would mean the rest of us would be freezing our asses off all weekend and he only gave us a few day's notice. To me this was the last straw, he hadn't been pulling his weight with a commitment to the show in months and I didn't feel he deserved to be an equal partner with Mick and myself as we were doing all the hard yards.

I tried to call Chris but he wasn't answering so I put a message on our group chat saying it was time for him to let us know if he was still 100% in or wanted to play a more minor supporting role in the crew. Again Chris cracked the sads and sent back a similar message as before along the lines that "He cannot work with me anymore and was stepping away from the project if I was going to continue being involved". That was the typical ultimatum that Chris was known for, it worked against Glenn but this time I was determined to call him out on his bullshit.

The next day I visited Mick at his work to discuss the future. Upon arriving I was a bit taken aback that Mick said he couldn't do the show without Chris. I even suggested Steph take his place in a more prominent role but that was shut down immediately. I dropped off the new camera and hard drive (containing the filming archives) and said I was going to get lunch but I drove home and quit the show. I received calls from others but nothing was going to work because they considered Chris more important than the person who created the show. I was disappointed in everyone and I offered to return if we could sort something out but it was a resounding no all round. After my obligations were done I said goodbye and signed away my ownership of Oz Fish TV under extreme duress from Mick saying he needed it in writing. I mailed him my resignation and ownership and I was so mentally messed up that I didn't care at the time.

At least I automatically still had "moral rights" which meant I legally had to be credited as the creator on all current and future broadcasts and seasons. I was happy enough with that and was already planning a live broadcast panel-type show with Glenn, this time focusing on ways that fishing can help those struggling with mental health issues. I had a breakdown a day or so later though when the police arrived at my door to hand me an interim intervention order prohibiting me from contacting Mick or Chris or writing anything about Oz Fish TV on the internet. I was stunned to read all these made-up allegations and decided to fight it in court the following month. I found out it is quite common for business partners to abuse the intervention order system to terminate or silence a partner. As Glenn told me "Grown adult men trashing a law that was set up for real threats of harm" referring to Mick and Chris. They were now ego maniacs high on their bullshit thinking they were famous rock stars or something.

Chris would put ridiculous posts up on the Oz Fish Facebook page claiming that their ratings weekly were the same amount of people watching that could fit into the MCG (Melbourne Cricket Ground can hold around 100,000 patrons). Talk about delusional. In response, I redirected their website to a gay porn domain while they continued to publicly bag me over the web to which I was unable to respond to legally. I then deleted all the Oz Fish domains and was ready for my day in court.

My parents were due back home from their two-month holiday in Europe and a week before they arrived my last grandparent passed away from a long battle with dementia, which also had taken her husband about a decade prior. I remember late into that night crying my heart out and I felt something I had not felt for a few years. I went to my guitar and wrote the music and lyrics in around thirty minutes. It just flowed out of me and I felt elated that my songwriting gift was still there. I recorded it and it was played at my Gran's funeral the day after my parents returned home.

About a week before my court date I was again visited by police for another bullshit and fraudulent intervention order from Stuart Maconachie, the skipper on the Mornington charter vessel. This one stunned me beyond belief because as far as I knew he and Sandra were on my side. It seemed they had thought that me trying to call them daily was viewed as harassment, yet all I wanted was a chat with my last friends. I've never known such a bunch of cowards in my entire life. Grown adult men taking out intervention orders so you cannot talk to them. I was completely disgusted with them all and my BPD issues, not yet counseled to understand it, made me have ideas of sinking his stupid boat at the pier. I think that is a normal human reaction, the difference is I did not do it, but I would have celebrated with an impromptu party if it did happen!

The court date arrived and I had to drive to Dandenong Magistrates Court and wait for legal aid. I received the dumbest lawyer on Earth saying I have to accept it because I re-directed their website to a gay porn page. I said no way in hell and questioned him about how he passed the bar test to even get a practicing certificate. He said thank you for your time "Sir" so I replied with the usual "No hard feelings...you dickhead. Fuck you". So I had to represent myself and even though the judge was respectful of my pronouns, she also was probably the second dumbest person in the building. I gave in after the judge warned me about contempt for constantly interrupting her and she was very annoyed that a business partnership was again in front of her seeking intervention orders.

I said I will agree to it but I want my video archive that was on my hard drive back. They handed it to me but told me it had been formatted. I didn't accept it and walked out not agreeing to any court order made in my absence. Got in my car after spitting on their windscreens, cracked a can of beer open and raced off home while chatting to Glenn on the phone. The legal system of intervention or restraining orders was being abused and misused severely and I felt the world had turned against me.

Mick, Chris and Jesse still had a couple more surprises for me over the next few months that would ultimately destroy me and send my body into shutdown with chronic depression and zero self-worth. The police tried over the next few weeks to serve me the final intervention order paperwork but I refused to answer the door. I was starting to despise the legal system and even set booby traps along the driveway to alert me of anyone entering the property. Eventually, the police served me the paperwork after recognising me walking down to the bus stop, so I removed the booby traps and wiped my ass with the order.

After seeing my new doctor at the Prahran Market Clinic, I felt it was time to do a mental health plan and to stop self-medicating as it was destroying myself and my family. I was put on Natraxone which is an opioid blocker that removes any desire to continue drinking even after one sip. It worked so well that I was feeling like a new person plus my counseling sessions were starting to open my eyes on how to learn to manage BPD.

The morons at Oz Fish still couldn't let it go. They had me criminally charged for breaching their intervention order. I was at the Melbourne showgrounds at the fishing and camping expo to visit Glenn as he had a stall there. Channel 31 also had a stall there and the Oz Fish "mega-famous superstars" were there. A part of the order said I was not to go within 400 meters of their workplace. I didn't even know they were there but Chris, the consummate smartass, decided to walk past me with my back turned and take a selfie of himself a few metres away from me.

Glenn later told me the whole crew was there and also videotaped the setup. The result was a visit from the police and a charge brief to attend Dandenong court, this time on criminal charges punishable by up to two years imprisonment. I hired an intervention order specialist lawyer named Glenn Thexton who was well respected and feared by police for his winning rate and was one of the best in Australia. He would later go on to expose the "Lawyer X" Nicola Gobbo corruption alongside Zara Garde-Wilson. I got on great with Glenn and after explaining the story he said he loved my television show but the new season was not as good.

After and six-hour wait just before the daily court sessions terminated, he came out of the head prosecutor's office and said "Let's go". All charges had been dropped and an apology from the head prosecuting police officer. Oz Fish was picked up by a few other networks including channel 44 in Adelaide and Aurora on Foxtel. Even the Australian Fishing Network (AFN), which was the biggest distributor of magazines, DVDs and mainstream media outlets, took it on board as an online streaming series.

But another kick in the teeth was about to happen. They cut

off the end credits to now read "Produced by Jesse Hommelhoff" with Michael Del Marco as the editor. I could not believe what I was seeing. All my thirteen episodes of season one had zero mention of me. I knew this was highly illegal and a case of stolen intellectual property and fraud. I still had legal "moral rights" and needed to be credited correctly for that season and every season to follow. What a disgusting act, but there was more to come from these oxygen thieves. I recorded the entire false-credits each week as evidence for my intellectual property lawyer who was giving me advice pro-bono after a recommendation from my former university lecturer Dr Kevin Purcell.

Then Oz Fish dropped another classless act by trademarking the name and the logo that I designed. By the time I found out it had already been approved. I never have known such human filth and perhaps this book may serve as their karma so many years later. The rights I signed away had zero merit and any contract lawyer would laugh at it. Their mistake cemented that by offering me no remuneration for work done and an agreement signed under extreme duress. It was invalid as my lawyer said and made worse by their public broadcast efforts showing misrepresentation by changing the credits, so I had a strong case for litigation. But with a starting price in the tens of thousands, I couldn't pursue it. At a rough guess, I would say I would be owed in the hundreds of thousands by Oz Fish TV for earnings lost, complimentary gifts such as kayaks, boats, resort holidays and the fact they committed and still do continue to commit fraud and misrepresentation because I created the show. They would still be sitting on a pier if it wasn't for me.

That's also another lie when the subject of piers comes up. On radio and podcasts, Mick and Chris claim they came up with the name Oz Fish TV and the concept while fishing together on Mornington Pier. Now their lies are exposed to the fishing community and executives on television networks, maybe they will have to go back to sitting on a pier as opposed to jet-setting around Australia spending my royalty money thanks to Channel 7. I have all the graphics, early video footage and other intellectual property "time-stamped" which shows they were not even involved when I created the concept.

The original credits & the fake credits

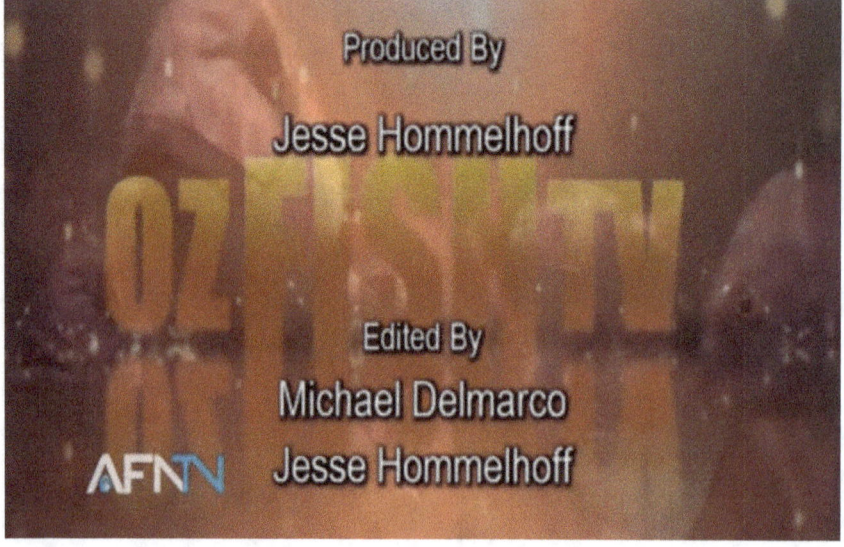

CHAPTER 10

THAT'S THE THING ABOUT FISHING

As my overall health started to improve I eventually decided to do a brand new show again with Guru Glenn and his friend, a Kiwi called Brian Rowley, or Nui as he was nicknamed. We decided to focus not so much on the fishing techniques as every other show was doing, but to do it more as a real-life show focusing on using fishing as a hobby or therapy to treat mental health issues and disabilities. I also wanted to add more of a journey feel to each episode and edit it into a more reality-based concept.

As a fan of reality shows like "The Kardashians", "Jersey Shore" and "Vanderpump Rules" I began a journey that would take my production skills far beyond what any other fishing show was doing. I wanted a world-class production and throughout the next few months, I gave it a damn good shot editing a monthly special and eventually creating Australia's first-ever live weekly fishing show broadcast in the style of a round-table panel discussion idea. Channel 31 wouldn't touch anything I did so it was all on

YouTube as well as the creation of my streaming network called "Fisho TV".

"That's The Thing About Fishing" is a term Glenn would always use as a reasonable excuse for catching or not catching fish, so at the suggestion of his partner Amy, we decided to go with that as the show's name. Three monthly specials that ran anywhere from an hour onwards. My editing style had become untouchable in the fishing TV community. Nothing was close to it, not even iFish with Paul Worstelling and certainly not those clowns at Oz Fish. I also started a weekly live broadcast from the Bell Marine factory starring Guru Glenn, Nui, a newcomer Karl Zomlye and regular caller to the show "Spiro from Broadmeadows", who was an employee at Bell Marine taking the piss out of any guests we had on the show.

The production of the live show was limited to three set-and-forget webcams and me on computer cueing segments, commercial breaks, and fishing reports. Each Wednesday Karl and I would go to a new fishing location and chat to the public on a segment that resembled Sam Newman's "Street Talk" on channel Nine's "The Footy Show". Lots of laughs were had and then I would quickly go and edit it all down for the show at 7.30pm that same night. We did ten episodes leading right up to the final Christmas special, but it was becoming too much for me mentally after an incident with Stuart the day of the second last show.

As part of his intervention order, I could not go within 400 meters of his workplace which was his boat docked at Mornington Pier. I had been going there a few times and would always make sure his boat was out doing a charter, so legally I was allowed to fish there. One day before the show was to air that night, he suddenly approached me. His boat had come in but I couldn't see it. The idiot tried to get a rise out of me by calling me derogatory names, so I gave him the finger as he walked off and noticed his deckhand was filming the incident from afar. They had set me up big time so I approached the foolish deckhand and said stop filming as I put my hand over the lens. She ran off hysterically overacting and I got charged with assault. That is a shit legal system for that to be considered assault. I got fined $600 with no conviction for breaching an intervention order. I had no lawyer just a Legal Aid counsel and just wanted it all over. This is purgery if you have to say you are guilty in court because Legal Aid won't represent a not-guilty plea unless it is inevitable you could go to prison. Fuck them. I did nothing no other regular human would do and I will never be sorry for that!

My world was now shattered again as I de-transitioned and threw away my entire female wardrobe. I ended all my friendships and cared about no one, not even my family. My BPD was not being managed well and I was drinking again secretly. My body was shutting down and I crawled into my bed at my parent's house for the next year barely eating, showering once a month and sleeping twenty-plus hours a day. When I was awake and my first thought upon coming out of slumber was always "Damn it I'm still alive". I was done with the world and done with myself...

The next year passed quicker than you might expect. When you have given up and your body and brain switch off, then sleeping passes the time even though the act of sleeping was constantly giving me the most horrific nightmares you could ever imagine. I hoped I would pass away peacefully in my sleep and was taking Restavit sedatives like they were out of fashion. I just did not care about anyone anymore. I had nothing more to live for and the damage called "my life" was telling me to fade away and make everyone more at peace with my crap not being dumped on their plate. I remembered that Brian Wilson from the Beach Boys once spent a few years in bed and I thought that was the silliest thing I had ever heard, but here I was at that same place. I just didn't have the talent or success he had and I felt like no one cared.

"That's just Ash being Ash" is what I presume everyone thought. I hated the world. I had given it so much love and creativity and I felt I was owed something. Not one of my friends, former friends or family can name a song I have written even to this very day. That has and always will bother me. Just because someone is famous and has a record deal does not mean they have talent. There are far more musicians out there a million times more talented than most chart-topping artists. They just haven't had their lucky break or gone down on their knees yet!

This was the first of the two times I have de-transitioned. Neither because of me, but solely a reflection of mental damage delivered to me by society. That entire time was a blur and felt like it passed in a blink of an eye...

On the set of "That's The Thing About Fishing" at Bell Marine

CHAPTER 11

FINDING THE TRANS COMMUNITY

In mid-2016 my parents went overseas again on a well-deserved holiday and I was starting to improve with my depression after starting to see a psychologist at the Prahran Market Clinic. Many light-bulb moments went off as I learned about my borderline condition and that there was a way, over time, to manage it without self-destructing so often. My psychologist was also a specialist in gender dysphoria, which sometimes crosses over into BPD and I was ready again to make another attempt at my gender transition.

I decided I wanted to try going out dressed as my true self to somewhere where others like me might be able to offer some support. After doing a bit of research online I decided to try DT's which was an LGBT pub in Richmond, but I wasn't sure what to expect. As I walked in wearing my little black dress I met a few trans girls including someone who seemed to be somewhat of the matriarch of the weekly gathering there, introducing herself and saying hello to everyone while snapping a selfie with all who were present. We would later have a major falling out and as usually expected from such former friends, she publicly started to refer to me as "he" and "him" which seems to be the dagger all people go for, even within the "trans community". My response online was equally as bad telling her to "Buy some toothpaste and Listerine for that halitosis". I felt bad for stooping that low but she had no right to misgender me, it's far worse when a trans person deliberately does it to you. I attempted to repair that former friendship many times but "she" still won't respond in any type of positive way. Sometimes my empathy for humanity, which is another aspect of BPD, can feel and be unrealistic and that's still something I struggle with even after years of counselling.

By the end of that first night out I felt right at home and had even had my first passionate kiss with a man which enhanced what I thought it felt to be a woman. I could not believe how nervous I was to sit next to a guy with my legs crossed like a lady wearing my little black dress and strappy high-heels and hair and makeup en-pointe. I looked into his eyes followed by my eyes shutting as we kissed. I felt so womanly and, although downstairs nothing worked anymore, my insides were so receptive that I wanted him inside of me, even if just to have the feeling of what I thought it was to be a female, although plumbing-wise very different.

It was many years later that I finally lost my virginity, but the feelings were so similar with butterflies and fireworks going through my body. The look in his eyes and being penetrated with my legs wrapped around him and his gentleness and masculine passion made me feel incredibly feminine that I could not wait to have my own actual vagina so I could experience sex as I imagined it while he was inside of me. It was the cuddling afterward that was so tenderly beautiful, just to have a man's arms around me and fall asleep together affirmed my dream that someday I might be able to afford to have my birth defect corrected. I will never be able to menstruate or have a baby grow inside of me and I hate God for doing that to me, even though there is no god.

I have even had serious, researched thoughts about cutting my thing off, geographically very close to a hospital and without anesthetic, but I was too scared of bleeding to death before actually making it through to the emergency entry. I doubt I will ever be able to afford any of the many surgeries but I would rather have nothing there if that was the last resort. I don't need or want it. I sit down to pee so WTF did I have to be born with this disgusting appendage that has ruined my life...

At DT's, everyone was so welcoming and friendly and it was definitely a confidence booster that I needed to fully pursue my next attempt at full-time transitioning. I was looking forward to doing it again the following weekend, however it took about six weekly visits for me to get banned from the venue for smuggling in booze disguised a water bottle. I got drunk that night and passed out but the owner just dragged me outside and left me unconscious on the sidewalk with no attempt at any responsible "duty of care". I was woken up by the police who were doing their job properly and making sure I was somewhat okay.

I was sent home in a taxi but didn't realise the owner had gone through my handbag and discovered my stash, so upon arriving the following weekend I was asked to leave. I found out these facts from an employee and former drag queen Rita the following week. Eventually that owner/tosser left and new owners came in and I was allowed to return about six months later but I was getting over it and was finding it harder and harder to relate to these trans girls that only dressed up on a Saturday night while I was living it 24/7.

We all have a different path I guess, so I'm not bagging anyone's journey, it's just hard to relate when I cop shit every day but they play it safe by only visiting places that are much more affirming than the reality of everyday life living as a transgender woman. Being part of several online groups at that time meant I now had more options, so I started meeting up with other trans girls at alternate venues like nightclubs and house parties. This is where I met Mishly who in her former life was an award-winning songwriting musician and was trying to find her way between going out weekly and the possibility of going "full-time", I get not everyone can afford to sacrifice their daily life, in particular their income, to pursue a better life as their true selves. For me, I just didn't care enough about a career or money to justify being miserable and wondering "What if?"... In saying that though, I can be a bit of a walking contradiction because "yes I have de-transitioned twice in my life" and "No I'm not happy presently, but I am happier overall". Mishly and I are still very dear friends to this day and although she is still struggling in her journey, I consider her one of the very few mentors of integrity, thoughtfulness and virtuosic musicality in my current life...

In late July I was excited to travel overseas to Bali on my first holiday as my authentic self. Nightly I would be a frequent visitor to the club scene in Seminyak where I made good friends with the staff and would hang out during the day with Damien, a sensational Michael Jackson impersonator who worked there. He would often give me a lift back to my hotel on his Vesper motorbike at 3am and I was grateful for that, because one night when he was performing in Kuta, I got robbed in an alleyway that adjoined my hotel and the main strip in Seminyak. Two guys on a motorbike flashed right by me and snatched my very dainty thinly-strapped handbag.

It was a bit of a spoiled night because up until that point I had been bar-hopping with a group of Australian girls as we danced, drank and flirted with guys. One Balinese guy took me to the bathroom and we pashed for a while before I went down on him. My new girlfriends saw how much I was beaming as I went back to join them for some more dancing. Then of course an hour or so later is when the unfortunate incident happened.

It was a lovely two-week getaway and the Balinese people are so warm and friendly. My days were usually spent shopping and trying out new food items and sitting at the beach watching the sun go down with about a thousand other tourists. It felt very liberating to be able to wear my one-piece swimming costume and a sarong with my hair French-braided by one of the local women. The sunset was incredible and I was hoping that maybe someday I could live in such a beautiful paradise.

A week after arriving back home I had a major accident at a nightclub called "Sircuit" on Smith Street in Collingwood. I had been dancing with new friends that I had met as well as playing the odd game of pool. We were all drinking but steadily pacing ourselves. At around 2am I said my goodbyes and went to leave. As I walked up a small incline ramp my shoe got attached to the sticky ground. I remember earlier in the night Amy, who I had just met, complained about how sticky the floors were. My knee crumbled to the ground and I fell thinking I had dislocated it which had happened before to wrestlers I knew. I tried to straighten it so it would reset back into alignment but I looked down and saw it was snapped in half and I could not get up at all. I started yelling for help and the staff and Amy came over to support me as we waited for paramedics to arrive. I remember laying there in a fair amount of pain as they loaded me up into the ambulance and off to the Royal Melbourne Hospital.

My stay over four days was quite an intense affair with every day being forced to fast in anticipation of possible surgery, but by the time it hit around 5pm, I would get the okay to eat because it wasn't going to happen. By the third day, I went into surgery where the surgeons wired my knee back together and stitched it up, but the pain upon waking was incredible. A good 10 out of 10 until the pain medication eased in and it then became a minus 10 out of 10. My leg was fully braced up with a solid velcro-style cast from my thigh to my ankle and upon getting discharged the next day, I had to learn to walk on crutches for the next eight weeks.

My social life was over for now and my self-esteem had taken a gigantic blow yet again. The next two months were agonising trying to cope mentally with being in bed all day, being unable to go anywhere and testing my parents' patience too with my constant complaining and deep depression. Just when I was at a major crossroads in my life with my transition, I got hit back down again and I decided to de-transition, De-transitioning is quite common and a lot of factors can mess with your state of mind to cause such a dramatic rewind in your gender journey. Gender dysphoria is different for everyone but one thing is for sure and it is that it never goes away and only time will solve the issue.

Mishly and me

The two Ash's, with Ashley Keller

My party crew back in the day

BACK TO GIGGING...

I ended up with a new found desire to return to music after attending a James Reyne concert and it was inspiring to know I could easily be up on a stage again like that. As I continued physio on my knee I hit the guitar hard again as I had not played seriously for many years so I was very careful in stretching and warming up to avoid re-visiting my left arm and wrist problems of the past.

In February the next year, it was time to put up or shut up, so I looked for a job as a lead guitarist through several ads on the internet. I got lots of replies but one, in particular, aroused my curiosity. I went and spoke to my brother Brad who had been working as an engineer and lighting specialist for "Staging Connections". I asked him which ones he had heard of. He pointed to one that he knew played regularly and was well-known in the cover band scene: "Shazam".

I got a message back with a phone number and had a chat with the band's leader Tony Silvano. He used the stage name Tony Jones because he used to do a massive casino act impersonating Tom Jones, as well as a past that included being one of the music directors at the old "Swagman" cabaret restaurant decades prior. We exchanged experiences and decided to meet in person the next day where he told me what was needed and if I was interested in auditioning the following Sunday.

That next Sunday I went to his house in Healesville. After a couple of cover songs, he said I was in and asked how quickly I could be ready to take over from their current guitarist whom he wasn't happy with. I asked when their next gig was and was informed it was this coming Saturday at a pub called "Beaches" in Mornington. Always a fan of throwing myself in the deep end I said "You want me for that one?" and they appeared a bit stunned.

I think that's the difference between professionals and people who do it as a hobby, a pro can be ready for a gig within days. So began the long hours of learning their catalog and that coming Saturday night I was a full-time member of Shazam. That year was full of regular gigs once or twice a week but Tony was trying to get away from the cover band scene which he had been on top of for over a decade by now.

We started rehearsing for an alternate band doing old 50s and 60s Rock 'n' Roll for the dance community, which had become a major stable of gigs for similar bands like the "Fender Benders". So we had two bands happening simultaneously: "Shazam" doing pub rock covers and "The Rockin Tones" catering to the huge dance crowd in Victoria. Eventually, Shazam would fade out, which disappointed me greatly because that was my true style and The Rockin' Tones would do on average around 150 gigs a year. In June of 2017 fate would intervene and I found a long-lost friend thanks to Facebook.

I hadn't heard from Jodie in decades, 25 years to be exact and suddenly I found her online. I was so excited as I had been trying to look for her all that time on-and-off and there she was. We began chatting over text messages for hours on end, like it was just a few weeks ago that we hadn't seen each other. She was my best friend and there she was living only a few suburbs away. I invited her to come down the following Friday to Club Kilsyth to see my band Shazam, which would be one of its last few gigs before we merged full-time into The Rockin Tones. She said she wasn't sure because of work and making sure her fifteen-year-old daughter was taken care of so I said no probs. I was just so excited to have her back in my life after such a long time.

Even after my entire gender journey I still had hope that it might go away if I found the right woman and here she was chatting to me. I saw what I thought was a real way out of my lifelong misery. That coming Friday while setting up for the gig, I looked over to see Jodie walking towards me. We had the biggest ever hug and I was absolutely over the moon to see someone from my past that I had such a connection with before the baggage of life started piling onto our backs.

She was in a very unhappy marriage with a man who was verbally abusive toward her and their daughter. So I guess I appeared at the right time in her journey to temporarily save her from his abuse. A few days later she visited me at my parents' home and we sat together to watch a movie. I had a feeling she might be interested in me so I just asked her and she grabbed my hand and said yes and we kissed. I could not believe it after so many decades of waiting to find her again and now there we were kissing.

I felt like I had been saved from my transgender torment and maybe I could have a normal happy life. But that was not going to be the outcome and I could feel my urge to transition again starting to return in time. We dated for about seven months and she went back to her husband to keep her daughter happy. I tried to see her one last time after I had a few too many drinks at a karaoke bar. She wasn't there but her stepdad called the police because he had no idea who I was or what I was going on about.

The police told me to go home as I walked away and hid in a bush down the street I waited until they left, hopped into my mum's car and booted it because I saw them head back down the road again. As I hit the freeway my tire blew out but I kept driving and eventually sparks were flying everywhere. I just wanted to get home and I finally made it only to have those same officers knocking at my door about twenty minutes later. They saw the car missing a tire and required me to do a breath test for alcohol on suspicion that I may have been involved in some type of collision.

I did not know that the law had recently been changed but I thought you could refuse a breath test if you were on your property, so I refused and called them every profanity you can think of. I thought I had gotten away with it as they left, but they returned two months later with an immediate suspension of my license until an upcoming court date. I fought it to the county court on appeal with Glenn Thexton as my lawyer again, but the judge came back after lunch and found a precedent from years ago that deemed me guilty. I was suspended for four years and I have never bothered or been able to afford to get it back. I'm glad that they caught me because I would have killed someone eventually and I feel so ashamed of my selfishness and the thousands of times I drove while drunk.

I now had to get a lift with other band members to keep playing and that became quite annoying for them over time. The Rockin Tones now had two new members: a new singer Leesa Farrugia and saxophonist extraordinaire Joe Breitenfeld and we were gigging two to four times a week. I became the on-stage music director and made sure all the vocal harmonies were right. It took a few months to get them sounding good and we were sounding like a very tight Doo-Wop old Rock n Roll band.

I also did the occasional gig with a rock cover band called "Exploded View" with Tony Anastasio on bass, Steve Howie on drums, Lexie Bright on lead vocals and Toby Beaumont on guitar. It was a sensationally talented band but eventually I had to leave because The Rockin Tones were getting so much work. Leesa left after about six months and I knew this was the beginning of the end. Things came to a head at a festival in Gippsland when Joe left because he couldn't deal with Tony, the band leader/drummer. I honestly was only sticking around to play with Joe because he was a world-class player and a musical mentor to me so I departed the band on the following day. I have not gigged since then and that was in February 2019.

By April I had decided to once and for all transition again and I had the dubious task of telling friends from my local pub the Blackburn Hotel. It did not go down so well for most of the patrons but there were a few people in my corner supporting me. I even got threatened to be beaten up, called "it" and "faggot" so it was just a matter of time before I left for good. I have found that the further you go from the inner suburbs the less accepting people are, maybe because their exposure to such things has been minimal, if at all.

The secret to my sound

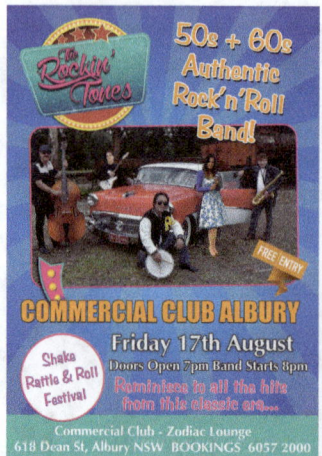

The Rockin' Tones

Ally & the Night Riders

Exploded View

CHAPTER 13

COVID PROTESTS

In March 2020, the world braced itself for the COVID-19 pandemic. Over the next few months things began to close due to government restrictions and eventually curfews. It couldn't have been worse timing for me. I had received a public liability payout from my knee injury and it would have been enough to pay for my gender reassignment surgery. Well, now that the world was in lockdown that wasn't going to happen so my loneliness was compensated by splurging on music equipment that I had never been able to afford previously.

I was living on a three-month lease on Flinders Street at the Aura apartment complex and besides having the odd "illegal" visitor, I was starting to lose my mind and spending money in huge amounts became my temporary fix. The no-win/no-fee law firm made off with the lion's share of my payout with their fee being well into a six-figure value while I got barely enough for a cheap house deposit at best. I bought a custom Ibanez swirl guitar, an Ibanez 7-string guitar, a cheapish 8-string guitar, and the last ever

Steve Vai Ibanez Prestige Jem (made in Japan) available in Australia before they discontinued production. I also got a new banjo and a hand-made sitar made by Waseem Maner in India as well as many other treasures that were nonmusic related like clothes, a tropical aquarium and a rare collector's ventriloquist doll of Gerry Gee from the 1960s in immaculate condition. I eventually sold it all once my money ran out, proving what an irresponsible fool I am with money.

As the last month approached until I would have to find a new home, I began getting deeply entrenched in researching COVID-19 and became exposed to the multiple websites and Facebook groups discussing the once-in-a-century plaque. I had way too much time on my hands and anger that my life-changing plans were being wiped out because of my solitude. I moved to St Kilda the weekend of the Dan Andrews (Victorian Premier) announcement of a six-week stay-at-home order and night-time curfew. I was about to slip into a giant rabbit hole that would consume my entire life and send me into a collision course with authorities.

What do you do when you cannot leave a room? You leave it anyway and hope you don't get caught which I did dozens of times, but it's the mental anguish that started to do my head in. I started researching conspiracy theories and joined multiple chat rooms on the encrypted phone app called Telegram where I would regularly speak with Morgan Jonas, Monica Smit, Steve Booth (aka Schteve Riley), Matt Lawson, Mel Ann and Bren Edgerton.

My days became consumed with "research" and believing eventually that the COVID "scam" was nothing more than the worldwide governments forming a police state, where we would be sent to concentration camps if we did not participate in compliance. After seeing Victoria Police manhandle so many hundreds of protestors online while I watched the live streams, I began to think of them as a version of the Gestapo. It sounds crazy writing this but that is what I truly believed and I was ready to join the cause at a higher level and fight for our lost freedom.

My first anti-mask/anti-lockdown protest was in October of 2020 and I made up fake credentials as a journalist complete with a legal sole-trader work permit, ID badge and the good old handycam from my Oz Fish TV filming days. It started around the Shrine of Remembrance and the police and protesters became extremely violent with each other. I would later find out it was the "Proud Boys" crew that were the ones trading punches with police. I followed the rest of the peaceful protesters on their walk to the bridge just before the Yarra River and Flinders Street station. I ended up on channel 7 news that night, the first of many times, with me pretending I was a journalist (face mask intact) and filming a scuffle between police and some old guy on the front line as they brought things back to order.

I felt sorry for the officers being a metre or so away, as they were mostly very young and you could see a sense of fear in their eyes, knowing that this could turn very bad at any moment if the thousands-strong crowd decided to break their line. My life now was 100% consumed with the COVID pandemic (or as we all called it "just a more severe case of the flu") and the harsh restrictions with growing distaste for the police. My sanity was being tested profoundly as I spent two months without any human contact while my paranoia and hatred towards those enforcing these restrictions increased to the point of planned suicidal thoughts. If I did not find a community I would have taken my life as a lot of people did during that time.

I found that community online and they had all become my new family. I attended all the other protests in the following months but it wasn't until February of 2021, when I met all these leaders in person at a snap-protest on Thursday the 18th at Flinders Street, that I became much more heavily involved and had nothing but utter contempt for the government, the police, Premier Dan Andrews and the mainstream media.

That night was a magical evening. I met Mel Ann at Flinders Street station and waited for the crowd to arrive. Dan Andrews had announced a strict lockdown again and as always we had a 7pm protest planned on any occasion that he announced such a quick shut down. I had called live on air to Tom Elliot at 3AW and invited his listeners to come and join us and his response was "I wouldn't recommend that because protesting is illegal during COVID restrictions".

That night around two thousand of us marched from Flinders Street to Rod Laver Arena as a show against the tennis being allowed to keep going while we were all locked up. Then it was a long walk back to Parliament House where I met up with Monica Smit and became her camera operator for the rest of the night. I also got to chat and march alongside Steve Booth (online name Schteve Riley) while he carried his enormous flag pole displaying the countries of England, the United States and of course Australia.

While the speeches started at the steps of Parliament, protected by about fifty police officers, an older guy named Bren sang a song called "We Are Coming" that he had written. I introduced myself as a fellow musician and suggested he record that song with a full band sound. He was a bit dismissive as he had just met me but within a couple of months, it was another successful collaboration and recording session.

I had no idea at the time that the protest movement I was involved with was mainly right-wing, but it was something I would discover in the ensuing months as I climbed my way up the ladder as a front-runner for each protest always making it on the national news on television and in the newspapers. One particular aspect of the right-wing involvement was run by a silly pseudo-religious group called the "Australian Peacemakers", run at that time by Nick Patterson and neo-nazi Jarrod "Jaz" Searby among others. They were just starting to make a tiny baby imprint on the leadership of the movement and it got me a little bit concerned as I knew that we were an anti-LGBT group with links to their original involvement with the "Proud Boys".

These people are a million percent on the ASIO watch list and some of their associate colleagues include Neil EriksonTom Sewell and Blair Cottrell. Three very extreme neo-nazis that would love nothing more than to bash the hell out of me or any trans person, but I kept getting most of the press and I imagine that pissed them off. A transgender woman keeps getting the majority of pics in the newspapers and film footage on the nightly news. I guess diversity can have its positive spin although looking back I think they let me march out front of the protests to dispel allegations of being right-wing bigots.

I imagine their train of thought must have been "No we don't discriminate, have a look at Ash out front carrying Schteve's three-flag pole". I didn't carry that pole until a week later but keep reading, the story has a while to go to fill you in on the events of the next week, which would involve serious illegal activity, imprisonment for someone and weeks of paranoia for me barricading my home with booby-traps and waiting for police and ASIO to knock my door down. This is how brainwashing for a belief works, you can seriously justify anything, perhaps even murder if what you believe is perceived as your truth. Absolutely anything, hence why a terrorist feels zero guilt for killing others. They believe they are in the right. That is what it feels like to be brainwashed...

On Saturday, February 20th, 2021 a protest was set for Fawkner Park which was about a ten-minute tram ride from where I was living in at the time. I got up later in the morning, had a few shots of vodka (aka liquid courage) and got ready as it was forecast to be a very warm day. Put a summer dress and sandals on (a big mistake if I knew how much walking I would be doing in the following hours) and chucked a vodka flask, purse, keys and Ventolin.

I remember rocking up there and quickly saying hi to Monica, Mel Ann and Raph Fernandez before deliberately obscuring the camera view of all the mainstream media by standing in front of their long lenses and moving once they did. it was like a game of baby chess for the next hour and I knew I had pissed them off in a major way. One even came up asking me to move and I pretended to talk in some pseudo-asian language not being able to understand just for my personal amusement in annoying him.

Member of Parliament Catherine Cummings did the first speech but got booed off the stage for asking us all to "socially distance" or the police would stop the gathering. There were hundreds of police already showing signs of kettling which is where they surround a group and pick them out violently one by one. The process had been used before on last year's Melbourne Cup Day in the city near the Parliament building. I was lucky I was sick that day so I didn't go, but the process of kettling and arresting each person on that particular day took many hours in the hot sun, with police not allowing anyone to even go to the toilet or access to water.

Monica gave a very emotional speech that day and I was very moved by her statement that she was willing to die for the cause. Then the storm troopers came in while people ran out to the main road led by Schteve with his flag pole. I tried my best to catch up but they were too far ahead. Once we turned the corner the police had completely barricaded any further access, so we had to turn back and return to Faulkner Park where reporters were running around trying to get their story for that night's news.

Police had set up another blockade so we were almost completely kettled in. I walked up to them feeling brave and tried to get through, then foolishly tried to perform a citizen's arrest on them. I was instantly put into handcuffs and I asked them to go easy because of my tendinitis wrist issues, but all it made them do was tighten them so my hands became numb. I was taken over to the booking area and I refused a search or to give my name. The group of male cops sitting and resting looked like something from a future science-fiction army and they were giggling at me. I was nothing but a guy in a dress to them and my rage resulted in me calling them every swear word you could ever imagine with zero fear of charges or detention. Eventually, I gave them my name so I could get released pending a possible five thousand dollar fine in the mail.

I went back in, getting in the police's faces again, right up the front line near Schteve as he called them "Nazi dogs". The police had lost their kettle line and you could see panic in the faces of the younger members. I even got kicked so hard in my calf that I could barely hobble as I walked off with Schteve to see him off to his car. What a day this had been and yes I was indeed on the national news that night, interviewed briefly by Channel 7 reporter Paul Dowsley.

The next day started with an online chat with Schteve and he had a plan for that Sunday night during the Australian Open tennis final. The plan didn't work and I knew that it wouldn't succeed upon arriving to meet him outside of Rod Laver Arena, although we did get up to some illegal antics that night which police are very well aware of courtesy of me when I defected from the movement many months later. If his plan had worked it would have been worldwide news and something no one has ever done before, so I shall leave it at that.

A few days later Schteve was arrested by the terrorism division of the police for using a slingshot to smash the front office window of Dan Andrews. He had been on their radar now for months and he was caught because police recognised the distinctive style and colour of his shoes on CCTC footage. He was remanded in custody for about sixteen or so days and in solitary confinement because of COVID requirements. No one heard a thing from him for many months and I imagine that the stress of being alone in your thoughts and away from his wife and two young children would have left him a partially broken man.

On March 20th I attended another protest, this time at Treasury Gardens near Parliament House and the place was swarming with police. I said hello to Monica and Morgan while and Bren Edgerton got up to sing a couple of songs on his acoustic guitar with a sign attached to it saying "FREE SCHTEVE". I also had a decent chat with citizen journalist Avi Yemini and offered my services as a camera operator. We exchanged numbers and listened to the speeches while the Victoria Police Intelligence Unit got good footage of every person there. I even was a smart-ass and tried to block their view with their pathetic handycam, which surprised me having a much bigger budget than I ever had while using one to film my television shows.

Catherine Cummings was there again and we had a chat. This time the police let the protest finish without interruption. About a week later another smaller protest was planned in front of Daniel Andrew's office and I got a call from Avi to help him out filming that night. Bren showed up carrying Schteve's three-flag pole and I thought that was such an honourable gesture. Avi's cameraman eventually showed up so I wasn't needed but I did help Monica and her father set up the portable stage but was feeling a bit left out and insecure being transgender, in what I was slowly discovering a mostly right-wing movement.

I met Catherine a few more times at a nightclub in Footscray and we would discuss the situation with lockdowns and Dan Andrews in great depth. My birthday was held there in late March and I was really surprised and happy that she also attended the "Pride of Our Footscray" club to celebrate with my other friends. "Pride" has always been a very safe and welcoming venue run by Mat O'Keefe and a lovely mixture of LGBT and straight people. When we all first started attending years before it was hard to fill the room with patrons but as I now sit here and write this I can assure and recommend to you the reader that it is now a world-class venue as a pub, cocktail bar and night club.

Around April of 2021, I put together some backing tracks with my limited home studio for two of Bren's songs. I thought they might become an anthem for any of the upcoming protests. His original song "We Are Coming" turned out well as a rock song with drums, bass, and guitar from myself. He also re-wrote the words to "I Was Only 19" by an Australian band called Redgum, but renamed it "Bullshit 19". I produced the video clips for each song with Bren in front of a green screen and various protest clips shown in the background courtesy of fellow protester Marty Focker and a political branch called "Reignite Democracy Australia" run by Monica.

The songs got some great feedback from the protest movement and I was proud to be involved as a higher-level participant now, but that was all about to change thanks to that fringe organisation calling themselves the "Australian Peacemakers". My last few days in the movement were filled with extreme hatred towards police and utter contempt for the draconian measures now about to ramp up to an extreme level again.

Leading up to these last few weeks of my involvement I had started writing a novel based on a future that I saw as controlled by authorities and those that disagreed had to form an underground movement to fight back, so basically the same as John Connor did in the "Terminator" movies. It started with a technical manual titled "Anti-Police Protest Tactics" or something like that. I eventually deleted all traces of it but it was a well-researched booklet with topics like fake ID, disguises, booby-traps, high-grade lasers, fishing hook snares, remote control offensives with drones, flares, a huge section on how to get out of a kettling situation and various booby-traps. It was on the verge of being a terrorist manual aimed against the police, but in my mind it was just part of my novel.

I still have trouble coming to terms with the fact I wrote something and I don't want to mention any other topics from it in case some true nutcase decides to fulfill their stupid cause and hurt people for real. It was a chapter in a fictional novel but I sent part of it to my cousin Rachael Gaylor because she was also a conspiracy theorist like me, but didn't realise that her partner Sam was a member of the Australian Peacemakers. It was a huge mistake as I would discover less than a week after finally deciding the movement was not for me. The Australian Peacemakers claimed they were doing God's work by defending any member of the public against police during weekly protests and they did not like me at all because I was transgender, an abomination as described in the Bible..

Leading up to the events of May 29th, 2021 I barely had heard their name but my cousin Rachael and I regularly got into mild arguments because she thought my role in the movement was minimal at best. It seemed like a massive jealousy ploy and it was strange because she was one of my only few cousins, out of many dozens, who regularly spoke with me and encouraged me with my transition journey. The Peacemakers despise all LGBT people and I was starting to see a similar twist in the values expressed by the anti-lockdown movement.

Thursday, May the 27th there was another snap-lockdown announced so again we all headed in our thousands to Flinders Street station for the ritual 7pm protest. By this point and actually for a couple of months now, I had been out front of the marches carrying an imitation three-flag pole in honor of Schteve. We ended up at Parliament House again but I kept hearing reports about Nick Patterson making threats to police online and even threatening them on that night. He would work in such a way as to appear macho but without advertising an obvious intention. Here are some of his quotes:

"You have the right to punch police officers in the face even if they don't detain you" (an online video conversation discussing the self-defense statute)

"Now we might be terrorising the powers that be if we get organised and according to them we could be terrorists...but that's good, we want them to be terrorised" (an online video conversation)

"If the police do the right thing, the government does the right thing, there's not going to be a problem" (speech at Batman Park May 15th)

"They want us to react, they want us to be violent. And I tell you I will be violent if I have to be" (speech at Flinders St May 27th)

"What you've done justifies our response that's coming because we have grounds for it now" (challenging police, May 29th in North Melbourne)

So Saturday, May the 29th arrived and the police warnings were getting full on. A protest was set for Flagstaff Gardens around midday but it was now 100% illegal to be five kilometres from your home and the cops were promoting it as a "ring of steel" around the area. I carried my three flag pole in honour of Schteve again, broken down in thirds as it was a surf fishing rod and I made my way to the gardens after getting off at Flagstaff station. I quickly attempted to set up my flag pole but I barely made it one hundred metres before the police stopped me. They wanted to know what I was doing and I refused to answer and used the traditional conspiracy-theorist round of asking each of them for their names and badge numbers. I still tried to push past the police but was restrained and threatened with arrest. There was a picture of it in the newspaper the next day courtesy of the Herald Sun. To be fair the cops took it very easy on me and gave me a move on order and upon realising I wouldn't be getting far that day, I left to try and find any fellow protesters in other locations.

It wasn't long before I saw some others and they said they were meeting at a new location at the Queen Victoria Market so I ventured my way through the smaller lanes to the car park of the market.

I noticed one of the leaders of the protest Matt Lawson was there with about fifteen or so others. As I quickly assembled my flags I began walking towards the ensuing police unit that was walking sternly towards us from about 100 metres away. I was wondering why there was no chatting or for that matter any noise behind me. I turned around to realise they had all run off like cowards. A leader who had done speeches at rallies, organised and marshalled illegal protests, yet there he was scurrying off down a side street. I was in disbelief as I thought he was a stand-up guy, but then a light-bulb moment illuminated itself: I think I have been being used by this movement. I had been told they were mainly right-wing and possibly anti-LGBT but maybe they were letting me hang around so their defense could always be to critical journalists "We are LGBT friendly, see look at Ash on the frontline" as mentioned previously. Ironically less than two years later they were among those protesting their hatred towards transgender people alongside Posey Parker at Parliament House. Also there were the Peacemakers and Neo-Nazi crowd led by Tom Sewell who would love nothing more to wipe people like me from the planet.

While the officers questioned me I kind of "gave it all up" at that moment. I was so stunned at how I had been betrayed that I fully co-operated with the police as they gave me a new move-on order. I called Schteve on my way home but didn't mention where my head was at now. He told me a major incident had occurred not far from where I was involving the Peacemakers, saying the police had assaulted and pepper sprayed them. The Peacemakers had been taunting police at Flagstaff and Nick Patterson thought he was outsmarting police by referring to precedents for freedom of movement, not having to identify etc. He had forgotten one major point in his pseudo-law-expert argument: "There were COVID directives set out as law during these times and it disqualified all legal context he was trying to make". Finally, the police walked towards the group to stop them from progressing and Nick and his followers just ran straight at the cops and went at it with fists and of course lost, with Nick receiving a broken shoulder. A bit of advice for anyone out there: Do not run at the police especially after you have just yelled at them "What you've done justifies what we're going to do because we have grounds for it now".

Schteve had been watching a livestream Facebook feed from Raph Fernadez and said it looked pretty full on. That was my final interaction with Schteve. After I left the movement he would often post transphobic memes on social media like "The only difference between tyranny and a tranny is Y" (obviously meaning why) and as a deliberate dig at me after my defection.

A few days passed until the police came knocking again. This time they took me into custody temporarily and interviewed me about a conversation I had had with my cousin Rachael and I couldn't believe what I was reading and seeing. She had given a copy of my "booklet" to the police electronically and as they showed me parts from it I was shocked at how far I had fallen down the rabbit hole. Suddenly my most supportive cousin had written a statement referring to me as "he" and "him" and I knew her partner Sam from the Peacemakers was probably involved. There can be a lot of jealousy among those groups regarding media attention and she was probably annoyed that I kept getting in the newspapers as opposed to Sam, who was arrested alongside Nick Patterson for assaulting police. I was charged with various offences pending a court summons for indictable acts. I went home and my brain shut itself off as I spent many days in bed.

That Friday I got visited by two officers to hand me the usual letter warning me not to attend the forecasted protest the next day. I told them I had decided to leave that crazy cult and suddenly their stern looks turned into that of approval. An hour later I got a visit from two detectives concerned about the potential for violence tomorrow and I told them the same thing. Eventually I would correspond with them about some of the inner workings of the movement that I was still aware of.

The police officers who charged me taught me a valuable life lesson the prior few days before. They said, "Ash you are very intelligent, most of the people we deal with are not. You have a chance here to change and it's never too late". It finally dawned on me they were there to help me, their job was to help people and get them back into a life of not offending. It was funny how fast I had gone from being a cop hater to the realisation that they are mostly good people doing their job called law enforcement. They said they didn't necessarily want to go to the protests and also pointed out that there are bad apples in every line of work, but maybe I had been only watching the bad stuff portrayed on social media. I went home relieved. I had finally decided: "I am done"...

Me at protests & being arrested again and again

The protest leaders

ASHJACKSON

Office of the Assistant Commissioner
North West Metro Region
Tower 1, 311 Spencer Street, Docklands 3008

4 June 2021

Dear Protest Organiser,

I write to highlight the current Chief Health Officer (**CHO**) restrictions that apply in Metropolitan Melbourne under the State of Emergency declared under the *Public Health and Wellbeing Act 2008* in response to the COVID-19 pandemic. The Acting Chief Health Officer Professor Allen Cheng issued the Stay at Home Directions (Metropolitan Melbourne) (**Stay at Home Directions**) on 3 June 2021.[1] You are only permitted to leave your home for one of the specified reasons in the directions.

Because of the risk of virus transmission where individuals gather in groups with others, the Stay at Home Directions prohibit both private and public gatherings. Specifically, clause 11(6) prohibits a person in Metropolitan Melbourne from 'arranging to meet, or organise or intentionally attend a gathering, with any other person for a common purpose'.

As a consequence of this restriction, it is not currently permitted for you to gather with others in a public place. This includes gathering at vaccination hubs unless you are attending the hub to receive a vaccination, either by appointment or as a walk in.

If Victoria Police determines that you are not attending a vaccine hub to receive a vaccine, then you may be breaching the Stay at Home Directions.
The penalty for breaching the gathering restrictions during the Stay at Home Directions is an infringement of up to 30 penalty units ($4956.60). You will be liable for this infringement if you do not leave the public gathering when asked by Victoria Police.

I urge you to remain updated with and comply with the Directions in the interests of public health and safety and encourage you to consider the advice from the Victorian Equal Opportunity & Human Rights Commission regarding the lawful limitation on a person's right to protest during lockdown (https://www.humanrights.vic.gov.au/resources/explainer-protests-during-covid-19/).

Yours Sincerely

Luke Cornelius APM
Assistant Commissioner North West Metropolitan Region

4/6/2021

---

[1] You can find the full copy of the Stay at Home Direction at this website - https://www.dhhs.vic.gov.au/sites/default/files/documents/202106/Stay%20at%20Home%20Directions%20%28Metropolitan%20Melbourne%29%20-%203%20June%202021%20%28signed%29.pdf

CHAPTER 14

LUCKY LANCE

Over the next few months I corresponded with a detective regarding issues and my knowledge of the "anti-everything" movement. Every couple of weeks I would get a visit from the officers that interviewed me to drop off paperwork, but more importantly they checked up on me to see how I was doing. That impressed me greatly and was the last nail in the coffin for me to 100% disassociate with that cult. If they didn't show that concern then I imagine I might have eventually started looking at conspiracy theories again and fell back down the hole.

The charges were all dropped once the case got to court about a year later and my cousin looked quite foolish as my lawyer tore apart her accusations as nothing more than a family squabble, all the while accusing me of things while sabotaging that by referring to me with deliberate incorrect pronouns and egging me on to reply to her so I looked like the bad one. The prosecutor who dropped all the charges wished me well and he hoped I was doing better. It was time to move on but we were still in COVID times so I temporarily moved back to my parents' home and began to heal from the effects of the brainwashing I had endured from by others, but mostly by myself...

By late June to early July, I was starting to heal a bit from the mental damage inflicted on me for such a fake cause. I kept hearing online about this guy that was intensely pissing off the people I had once stood with at protests and was calling them out for the scamming that they were doing, which I was very much unaware of. His name was "Lucky" Lance Simon and he had a sordid history himself, having been involved most of his life in crime and even acquitted of murder a decade or so prior, but had turned his life around and got married and had children. I thought I would visit his social media page and see what he had to say as all I heard previously from my prior cult days was how much he was hated and even rumours about exacting revenge on him.

I was quite surprised at how entertaining and charismatic he was in his videos. So I reached out and sent him a private message explaining that I used to be deep in the anti-everything movement, and he replied almost instantly asking if we could have a phone chat. We spoke for ages while I told him my story and over the next few weeks we became quite good friends, as I discovered how these people I once marched with had various ways of scamming followers out of thousands of dollars which combined would add up to many millions.

The basic principle of how they scam people is always through some interaction with the police. You record an incident where you are argumentative with them, trying to get a reaction that will offend them. Once charged by the police they then "grift" for legal fees way above what representation in court would cost. The term "grifting" means setting up a donation page, explaining the incident in their favour and asking for donations to fight the charge in court using a dodgy barrister who was probably in on it to begin with. Some would raise $50,000 to $200,000 for a matter that might cost $5000 at best and they pocket the rest.

Scam #2 is somewhat a bit more legitimate but still dodgy ethically. You film your interaction with police, drag the incident out and annoy them to the point that they have a somewhat entertaining edited video clip to post to a platform like YouTube. Then with monetization on the amount of views you get, which is roughly $10,000 per million views, you can make a nice paycheck. A lot of the people doing this, in particular Simeon Boikov (aka Aussie Cossack) became semi-famous in the movement but their egos would usually cause them to mess up and breach the terms of YouTube and eventually get banned. I think that moron is still in hiding at the Russian Embassy after he live-streamed himself assaulting an elderly man and a warrant issued for his arrest, probably delusionally thinking he is a now a political prisoner like Julian Assange.

Avi Yemini, another Melbourne based citizen journalist, is an expert at "grifting". I found some videos by commentator Tom Tanuki and Lucky Lance online demonstrating his attempts at convincing his followers to donate their hard-earned cash to him through a dodgy news outlet called "Rebel News" based in Canada with Yemini being the Australian correspondent. His campaigns to "fight the COVID fines" which took in hundreds of thousands of dollars, never required a lawyer to that amount, but pocketed the rest which is a standard scam in the grifting business.

On Australia Day a couple of years ago, he made a video live from the back of a police van claiming he was under arrest. This has been a main stable for Avi as he rocks up every year on that day to offend protesters and get footage of their sometimes awkward and hostile reactions. The police know him all too well and this year, similar to previous years, he was given nothing more than a move-on order. The police consider him more like a pest and usually put him in their van, dropping him off a few blocks away with that same move-on order again and the warning that if he comes back, he will be charged with disturbing the peace.

"I'm now in the back of a police car and I've been arrested for what they alledge is a breach of the peace. The breach was that I attended the so-called invasion day to report and do my job. I came with my federal accreditation from the government"

(It was actually a press pass only valid in Canberra for interviewing foreign political visitors)

"I'm now being driven to an undisclosed location and I don't know if I am going to be charged. But I need your help. Please go to "rebelnews.com/freeavi" right now to help secure my freedom. I've got my gun lawyer Madeline on the case right now fighting to secure my freedom so I can go back and do my job...If you can cover the cost of my legal battle that I'm in right now then please donate"

The problem lies with the fact that someone monitoring the Rebel News website noticed this footage had gone online less than forty minutes after he live streamed himself in the police van. So in reality this page had gone up after the police had released him with the move-on order and Rebel News was promoting this "Free Avi" donation page to fight his legal battle when there wasn't a case to begin with.

But there was a much more damning nail in the coffin for Avi and Rebel News. A Twitter user scanned the logo of the "Avi Yemini

Arrested" banner and discovered the the image in question was made over five hours before according to the meta-data electronic fingerprint and created in North America by a member of Rebel News. That proves undoubtedly that Yemini and his Rebel News cohorts conspired hours before the arrest (which they knew happens every year on that day when he shows up at the rally) to create a donation page to crowdfund for a nonexisting legal case. If this wasn't true then why haven't Rebel News or Avi himself attempted to sue Tom Tanuki or Lucky Lance for breaking the story and exposing the scam?

After getting to know Lucky Lance a bit longer and seeing how much work he was doing behind the scenes to expose these scammers, we decided to meet in person and let the scamming/anti-everything movement know I had defected "live" on social media. I had been somewhat undercover during the previous month and assisting detectives with information about protests via the Telegram app but it was now time to declare my alliance with Lance.

We met up at Mordialoc Pier where I was fishing and he offered to drive me home. We made a stop on the way to film a video enlightening the movement that I had changed sides. We chose to do it out the front of a Masonic Centre just to rub salt into the wounds as the anti-everything movement and their Qanon theories believed the Masons are demon worshippers ready to make a New World Order and put in "the great reset" to reestablish society through a huge depopulation created through the "COVID hoax". There is no "New World Order" trying to take over the world, what benefit they have in reality of doing that? The wealth of the world and all underneath relies on everyone not so wealthy trying to their climb their way upwards, so to "eliminate them" would solve nothing! Anyway, to explore the NWO and Qanon theories would be another book in itself, one I am happy to explore, but I would rather focus on my journey first before trying to fully explain that deep dark rabbit hole in further detail.

We did a few takes and then I appeared on camera with Lance and was proud to do it, but the following weeks I received threats which I would consider ranging from extreme violent attacks to death. They were always worded in a pseudo-threatening way with a fake account but I passed them on to the police. One threat said "Pliers, Blowtorch" and I replied "Talking about the movies Pulp Fiction or Chopper?". I have never and will never back down from a bully or a threat.

In the following protests after I left the movement the level of violence against police increased significantly. I was watching a livestream from Rukshan Fernando (aka. The Real Rukshan) and there was a stand-off with police as they had kettled a crowd of hundreds. Suddenly the police line was broken by techniques I wrote about in my anti-police book and almost simultaneously on Avi Yemini's live stream from a different location, the same thing happened. I was hoping that part of my book was not shared by my cousin but I am fairly certain the Peacemakers probably got given a copy from her partner Sam Cowley.

I saw a police officer knocked out cold with a coward punch from one of the protesters as they broke the line, another one taken down with some sort of MMA (Mixed Martial Arts) grappling move and flares being thrown at the police. This was a far sight different than when I was involved and I was stunned as these pretend citizen journalists would edit the footage later on to make it look like police were the aggressors when they would retaliate with pepper spray and rubber bullets to keep the mob of many thousands from full-on rioting.

My new mission was my alliance with Lance in taking down these fraudsters, so I would save all the protest live videos and go through them and identify who was doing what and would pass my findings onto detectives. Matt Lawson, the leader who ran away like a coward when I was with him and about to challenge the cops, complained the police were way out of line and showed Avi his injuries from the rubber bullets on his stomach which were nothing more than getting shot with a paintball gun.

In August of 2021 Monica Smit, leader of the political movement "Reignite Democracy Australia", filmed her arrest in her car as she was taken into custody for a few weeks on charges of incitement. Lucky Lance was over the moon and did a video praising Victoria Police and pouring an expensive bottle of champagne over his head while laughing like a maniac. He couldn't mention her name on camera because she and others had multiple intervention orders against him, which in time were all eventually thrown out of court. It was again sad to see such deliberate misuse of a court system just to silence a critic of grifting and Lance has probably had the most intervention orders in Australian history.

Except here is the catch, Lucky Lance has the time and he fights every single order against himself and has never lost in court with any final intervention orders ever granted. The consequence of lying in your statement and having your case heard and the discovery of your false accusations is...nothing! And during those months and years when Monica Smit, Avi Yemini and many others have filed them against Lance, he has had to remain silent while they bagged him and try to humiliate him publicly online. My hat goes off to you Lance!

Left: Lance celebrating another victory, the arrest of another grifter. Right: Ash joins Lucky Lance for a live video out the front of a Masonic centre. Bottom: Another victory in court against fraudulant intervention orders

CHAPTER 15

THE AGE

As the protests continued I mentally had to back away completely and by November of that year, I felt I had moved on from that unfortunate time in my life. I was now fully vaxxed and had moved back to St Kilda where two good friends of mine from the "Blackie" (Blackburn Hotel) were now also living. Emma had been there for a while and Brad, my pool teacher from Blackburn moved across the street from me about a month after I did. We called ourselves the "Three Amigos of St Kilda" and Brad, who had always struggled to find money during COVID thanks to his hospitality job, was back at work and appeared to have found a new true home. The three of us would hang out a few times a week and usually have more than a few drinks. He would often come over to my apartment and we would sit there and chat about life until he would fall asleep.

I was still in regular contact with Lance and he mentioned a journalist from "The Age" wanted to reach out and talk to me about my time in the anti-everything cult. I didn't want to revisit that part of my life. I had moved on as well as being offered a placement the following year doing my Masters Degree at the Australian Institute of Music. Lance subtly kept suggesting it might be a good idea to at least talk to the reporter and if an article is printed about my journey, it might help others get out of that movement. Around December I agreed, although still slightly reluctantly and Lance put me in contact with Rachael Dexter from "The Age" newspaper.

Over a few phone calls, I divulged my anti-lockdown/anti-everything journey and eventually in January we met in person to film some supplementary video footage for the online version of her upcoming article. I was still only a few weeks out of recovering from catching the COVID-omicron variation so my health was okay but certainly not in good summer health. I caught COVID at a New Year's Eve party and had been double vaxxed so I was saved from the life-threatening aspect of it, but it was pure hell for a few days. I was bedridden with an incredible fever made worse by weather temperatures being around the mid-thirties celsius and I had to crawl to get to the bathroom. Emma, Brad and my parents would drop food at my gate while my body was in shocking agony all over. After a few days it passed fairly quickly and the symptoms were that of a mild cold.

The filming segment for The Age article was a very emotional and draining few hours re-visiting my story in front of a camera with Rachael asking me sometimes very difficult questions, but I braved through it with honesty and the article was set for release a few weeks later, just as the uprising in Canberra of sovereign citizen protesters was at its peak against the government and it's COVID response in general. Here are some extracts from that article:

Falling into the 'freedom' movement ... and getting out
By Rachael Dexter (February 13, 2022)

At the height of Melbourne's anti-lockdown protests, Ash Jackson was a familiar face. Front and centre of screaming crowds, she dutifully waved flags, clashed with police and was arrested several times. For almost a year she was consumed as a follower of the 'freedom' movement – entire days were spent online, reading and watching anti-government videos and posts on encrypted social media apps, becoming increasingly paranoid, angry and obsessed. Jackson turned up on the news more than once after being arrested and shunned by family and friends. But now she's out.

About eight months after leaving the movement, she still can't believe the grip it had on her life. Jackson says if you had asked her a year ago where she might be in 2022, she would have said in a concentration camp for the unvaccinated or engaged in an insurrection after a communist takeover. "I was thinking by this time ... that we'd have an underground movement with weaponry," says the 48-year-old.

In her small Melbourne apartment, Jackson brings up a YouTube video on her television. It's a Channel 7 report from February 20, 2021, the day hundreds of protesters marched to the Shrine of Remembrance and ended up being corralled by police at Fawkner Park, where dozens were arrested. Amid the angry mobs, Jackson points to herself. That day, while attending the protest, she was arrested after marching up to a group of police to conduct a "citizen's arrest" of the officers for "crimes against humanity". "I was so brainwashed" she says as she watches the chaotic scenes, shaking her head.

The 'freedom' movement, initially centred around anti-lockdown and anti-vaccine sentiment, saw protesters take to the streets, particularly in Melbourne, every weekend for almost two years to reject COVID health measures. Last year, as lockdowns lifted, the movement's leaders shifted their attention to vaccine mandates. This year protesters have descended on Canberra, including on Saturday, talking about everything from the dangers of vaccination to QAnon-adjacent theories about paedophiles within the Australian government.

At the extreme edges are those who claim they are willing, as "sovereign citizens", to launch a full government takeover – violent or otherwise. In his latest annual threat assessment, delivered this week, the boss of Australia's counter-espionage agency ASIO, Mike Burgess, highlights growing concern about online radicalisation during the pandemic, noting vaccine mandates and lockdowns had fuelled extremism that is not "specifically left or right-wing". "More time in those online environments — without some of the circuit breakers of everyday life, like family and community engagement, school and work — created more extremists," he wrote.

Just before the emergence of COVID-19 in early 2020, Jackson was working part-time as a musician; composing music for productions, gigging around Melbourne's suburbs in cover bands and teaching guitar. Victoria's initial six-week lockdown drove her out of work. She had no real social interaction for more than two months. At home, scrolling on her phone, she found anti-lockdown groups starting to call out what they saw as overly harsh measures from an increasingly dangerous police state. "I stumbled across some things on the internet, and I was like 'Oh this makes sense, I don't want to be locked down'," she says.

She can't remember the specific video or post that first touched her conspiracy nerve, but she became a big fan of influencers such as Monica Smit of Reignite Democracy Australia – a lobby group backing Craig Kelly and the United Australia Party – Smit's partner, podcaster Morgan Jonas and Avi Yemini from Canada-based right-wing commentary website Rebel News. "I was slowly finding myself getting brainwashed," Jackson says. "I kept looking into conspiracy theories, including QAnon. I started rooting for Donald Trump, which was ridiculous. Being trans ... he's not very favourable to us." Once a born-again Christian, Jackson had left her faith over a decade earlier, ousted from her church for coming out as transgender. It was a deeply wounding experience she still has trouble talking about. "I've sort of been a little bit of a loner [since]," she says. "I found a bit of community in the anti-lockdown movement."

She became a regular on the front line at Melbourne's anti-lockdown rallies, coming onto police's radar for disseminating a handbook on how to thwart officers at protests. "I got sucked in big time to the point where I was doing ... very dodgy illegal stuff that I'm ashamed of now, but at the time I thought it was justified," she says. She's visibly distressed about the abuse she hurled at police on the front line. "I gave them so much shit, I called them every name under the sun," she says.

It was her experience with Victoria Police that planted the seed for her escape. In late May last year, at her last 'freedom' protest, she was encouraged by other protesters to throw herself in front of police after receiving a move-on notice. Police arrested her, while she says the others ran away. "I was kind of thinking, 'Where the hell are my friends?'" she recalls. "They all just buggered off and left me. "I was confused ... so I didn't give the police a hard time at all. And they said, 'Look, we're going to give you a move-on because you've been so cooperative'."

The following week Jackson was arrested at home and taken in for questioning over her role in the protests and the anti-police booklet circulating online. When the formal interview was over, she says officers spoke to her candidly about their life, their families, and how difficult it had been working on the front line during the pandemic, showing sympathy for her struggles with her gender and mental health. "I realised, 'These aren't the Gestapo or anything ... I had it all wrong'. "I had tears when I was just talking candidly with them just saying, 'God how have I f---ed my life up like this?'

Police didn't lay charges that day and offered Jackson a lift home. "I said, 'No, actually, I wouldn't mind walking. I need to think about my life'." Jackson went home and fell into a deep, days-long depressive spell, during which she self-harmed. By this point, she had lost ties with her extended family, had a criminal record, and felt she had been manipulated. Around this time she found others online who had grown skeptical of the movement and had begun questioning the extraordinary amounts of money being raised. This and follow-up welfare visits by the police were the final impetus for her to leave the 'freedom' movement. "The weight that came off my shoulders instantly – it was unbelievable," she says. "If I didn't leave, I would have probably ended up in some sort of psych ward or something. When you believe strongly in something and that the police are coming for you, the government's coming for you, you're going to get sent to a concentration camp. "I used to be in my apartment and I'd have the door barricaded with a couch and tables. I'd booby-trapped the windows. "It was consuming and eating me away. Just destroying my soul and my friendships – I lost a lot of friends." "And so it looks like people aren't just passive consumers of information. They're working towards finding stuff that makes sense to them or makes sense of the world for them."

Jackson says she is now getting her life back on track. She's recently moved house for a fresh start after a long period of recovery living with her parents and this week is going back to university to study for a masters degree in music. She recently recovered from COVID-19 too, a mild case she attributes to now being vaccinated.

She becomes emotional when she talks about her extended family, who welcomed her back at Christmas. "The biggest moving part for me was seeing my nieces," she says. "I didn't see my nieces for like eight months and I love my nieces. And just seeing them again was amazing." "I was expecting I was going to have to spend [Christmas] by myself and I got a call from my brother the day before and he said, 'You're more than welcome. What's in the past is in the past, and we're glad that you're safe and that you're out of that.'"

Ash still keeps an eye on the movement, which was responsible for a fire at Old Parliament House in December and has now set up a permanent camp at the Canberra Showgrounds with leaders claiming to stay put until the government is "cleaned out". Amid calls for an end to vaccine mandates and vaccine passports are speeches about the "paedophile cabal" by leaders who have repeatedly called for MPs to be hanged. Last week convoy leader James Greer, who raised almost $200,000 in crowdfunding for the protest, was arrested after police found a loaded rifle and ammunition in his car at the protest campground. "It's so different to what it was even a year ago," says Jackson. "I can fully see some sort of domestic terrorist thing happen." She believes most people will "have to hit rock bottom themselves" to leave the movement and hopes her story helps others. "I still care about some of these people, you know? I hope they can get out."

Rachael did a sensational job on the article treating it with clear solid facts and compassion and it was met with a positive response except for the anti-everything movement. In particular,

Monica Smit who wrote an online press release on the Reignite Democracy website playing down my role in the movement and trying to defend the negative vibe of the story towards her organisation, but she was positive in her overall comments of my character but never referred to me as any pronoun, just "Ash". She said I was welcome back to the Reignite family anytime. But I had other things on my mind, a few days earlier I had been to a funeral and my soul was feeling desperately crushed by the loss of one of my best friends. Brad was gone!

I remember him sitting on my couch a week earlier saying "Ash you are a real true friend"... I had known him for about five years after we met with his girlfriend Liz playing pool at the Blackburn Hotel. I had only just started playing pool and enjoying the solitude of practicing by myself and occasionally asking a stranger for a game. Brad and Liz were playing on the adjacent pool table and he asked where I played competition and for which club. Little did I know that was him joking with a deadpan face because I was shit at the game. He gave me some coaching that day in exchange for shouting him a couple of beers. Over the next few weeks we would bump into each other and he introduced me around to the locals. He worked at a restaurant as the manager about a street away and he and Liz both became good friends over time, even standing strong beside me when I transitioned again years later.

A couple of weeks earlier on Australia Day 2022 I saw him sitting on the steps of the local tram stop near where we lived in St Kilda and he was crying in pain. He had been going through extreme bouts of agony in his left shoulder for several months and claimed he needed surgery to fix damaged nerves but because of COVID, all elective surgery was on hold. I offered to take him across the road to the local clinic just to get seen because I was very concerned but he refused and I had to help him walk back to his home opposite my place. A few hours later he called me and asked if I could go to the local supermarket and get him a few things and so I happily obliged not knowing it would be the last time I would see him alive as he greeted me at his back gate to collect. Emma had spoken with him a few hours later that night and we thought it odd the next day when we left him messages to hang out after work but received no response.

The following morning I was at my parents and got a call from Liz asking me to check on Brad because she also hadn't heard from him either. I was in the car with my mum getting a lift back home when Emma called me saying she was at Brad's and the landlord was there about to open the room he was renting. All I heard in the confusion was Emma saying "Come here quick, I think he's hurt or might have passed". As my mum dropped me off I jogged as best I could through the pouring rain to Brad's place just as an ambulance and police were arriving. Emma was in the foyer and I asked what was happening and she said she didn't know because they wouldn't let her see him.

An officer came to us to inform us that he had passed away and I burst into tears as me and Emma hugged. We sat with the police as the paramedics asked us questions about him and his general health. My heart was crushed and I called my mum who had gone to see if Liz to was alright or even aware of what was happening. The sergeant informed LIz over the phone that Brad had passed and I broke down again, this time more concerned for Liz as she had just lost her mother to cancer a couple of years earlier and now her boyfriend too.

The rest of that day and the following days were a blur of tears mixed with heavy drinking and trying to comprehend how a forty-seven-year-old could die from a heart attack. The funeral was a disgraceful attempt by his family that he barely knew and it included no friends being asked to participate. We were the ones who knew him best. We were his family. I still feel like I had no real closure but as I sit here and write this with tears streaming down my face, I want to say thank you to you Brad for your friendship and the thousands of laughs and good times we shared. I wish you could have lived to know that I ended up a few months later working in hospitality just like you. Thanks for letting me win a game of pool occasionally too. Farewell, my friend...

Falling into 'rabbit hole'

From Page 21

report from February 20, 2021, the day hundreds of protesters marched to the Shrine of Remembrance and ended up being corralled by police at Fawkner Park, where dozens were arrested.

Amid the angry mobs, Jackson points to herself. That day, while attending the protest, she was arrested after marching up to a group of police to conduct a "citizen's arrest" of the officers for "crimes against humanity".

"I was so brainwashed," she says as she watches the chaotic scenes, shaking her head.

The "freedom" movement, initially centred around anti-lockdown and anti-vaccine sentiment, had protesters take to the streets, particularly in Melbourne, every weekend for almost two years to reject COVID health measures.

Last year, as lockdowns lifted, the movement's leaders shifted their attention to vaccine mandates. This year protesters have descended on Canberra, talking about everything from the dangers of vaccination to QAnon-adjacent theories about paedophiles within the Australian government.

At the extreme edge are those who claim they are willing, as "sovereign citizens", to launch a full government takeover – violent or otherwise.

In his latest annual threat assessment, delivered this past week, the boss of Australia's counter-espionage agency ASIO, Mike Burgess, highlights growing concern about online radicalisation during the pandemic, noting vaccine mandates and lockdowns had fuelled extremism that is not "specifically left or right-wing".

"More time in those online environments – without some of the circuit breakers of everyday life, like family and community engagement, school and work – created more

The federal government this month announced it would commit more than $60 million to countering violent extremism amid an increase in conspiracy theories during the pandemic and concerns about MPs' safety, and on Wednesday the Victorian Greens secured a parliamentary inquiry into the growing threat and influence of far-right extremism in Victoria for the same reasons.

But another complex problem has been left in the pandemic's wake: the path back for thousands of individuals whose lives, livelihoods and personal relationships are in tatters after going down the rabbit hole of these conspiracy theories.

While the path is different for each person, experts and former conspiracy theorists say an urgently need to better understand why and how this descent happens.

Just before the emergence of COVID-19 in early 2020, Jackson was working part-time as a musician composing music for productions, gigging around Melbourne's suburbs in cover bands and teaching guitar. Victoria's initial six-week lockdown drove her out of work. She had no real social interaction for more than two months.

At home, scrolling on her phone, she found anti-lockdown groups starting to call out what they saw as overly harsh measures from an increasingly dangerous police state.

"I stumbled across some things on the internet, and I was like 'oh this makes sense, I don't want to be locked down,'" she says. She can't remember the specific video or post that first touched her conspiracy nerve, but she became a big fan of influencers such as Monica Smit of Reignite Democracy Australia – a lobby group backing Craig Kelly and the United Australia Party – Smit's partner, podcaster Morgan Jonas, and Avi Yemini from Canada-based right-wing

"I was slowly finding myself getting brainwashed," Jackson says. "I kept looking into conspiracy theories, including QAnon. I started rooting for Donald Trump, which was ridiculous. Being trans ... he's not very favourable to us."

Once a born-again Christian, Jackson had left her faith over a decade earlier, ousted from her church for coming out as transgender.

It was a deeply wounding experience she still has trouble talking about.

"I've sort of been a little bit of a loner since I," she says. "I found a lot of community in the anti-lockdown movement."

She became a regular on the front line at Melbourne's anti-lockdown rallies, coming onto

handbook on how to thwart officers at protests.

"I got sucked in big time to the point where I was doing ... very dodgy illegal stuff that I'm ashamed of now, but at the time I thought it was totally justified," she says.

Conspiracy theories are not new, but in the internet age they grow and morph quickly. Pre-pandemic, QAnon – a theory that the world is run by a cabal of paedophiles who drink the blood of children – was dominant online. Evidence from online support groups suggests that now the overlap between QAnon and anti-vaccination sentiment is strong.

One of the moderators of the 230,000-person Reddit page "QAnon Casualties" is Sydney man Jitarth Jadeja. Five years ago, he returned to Sydney from the

States and was living at home, studying part-time with no job or partner. He became thoroughly obsessed with US politics.

"I was really basically on my own on the internet just all day, every day."

He was shocked when Donald Trump unexpectedly won the presidential election in 2016. He questioned how it could have happened, searching for alternative media. Before long, he fell deep into the first-ever worldwide conspiracy theory of QAnon.

Eighteen months later, a series of high bulb moments made him realise QAnon was a "con". He wrote about this experience in a Reddit post which later went viral. He has since taken to talking open

THE PROJECT

After the article in "The Age" came out I received several offers from other media outlets including ABC "The Drum" as well as radio, but one in a pile of messages was from Channel 10's prime-time award-winning current affairs show called "The Project". I wanted to get this message out to as many people as possible, so that became my first preference as I replied and had a phone call with one of the show's producers. We agreed that doing a special segment would convey my journey with much more justice instead of sitting at the desk doing a live interview, in addition it would allow double the amount of air-time so the next day I was at channel 10 in South Yarra at the Como building where I met with the producer Georgia.

Because COVID was still around and gaining traction again from the Omicron variant, I was not allowed to get my makeup done at the studio so my dear friend Laura did it. The lighting was quite intense and overall I looked pretty ordinary even though she did do a sensational job on my face. The camera crew was absolutely miles ahead of anyone I had worked with at Oz Fish TV and Georgia was an absolutely lovely and compassionate producer knowing this was going to be a very hard thing for me to do.

As I touched up my makeup and sat down the host Waleed Aly came in and we had a brief chat. He was an A-grade celebrity, a Logie Award winner and a very intelligent and humble guy. We sat as he interviewed me for a good ninety minutes and then off-camera for about half an hour, sharing guitar talk as he was also a very talented musician as well as a journalist. I was not paid for anything by any media outlet including The Age or The Project and I would have refused even if anything was offered.

People needed to know there was a way out of conspiracy theories and cult-like organisations and I felt Waleed asked the right questions and added the right commentary to explain both sides of the anti-lockdown movement and the general public's response to them. After thanking and saying goodbye to Waleed, the remaining three of us (Georgia, the cameraman and myself) departed for a quick lunch then off to the city to film some supplementary footage at Parliament House and eventually back at my apartment.

As the days passed my anticipation grew and I was starting to wonder after a whole week if they had abandoned the story. Georgia apologised for the delay but they needed that extra time to get the segment perfect. She said if I wanted to pursue any other media that was fine so I did a radio interview on the ABC a few hours before "The Project" was about to put my journey live on national television.

Then just after 7pm, alone in my apartment with the television on and a nice cold beer in my hand, I awaited my television premiere. It was Wednesday the 23rd of February 2022 and the story was about to air. It was about my pain. About my loneliness and desperation to find a community that cared for me. Part of me wanted to turn it off and lock myself in my room for the next few weeks until it all passed. I didn't want the attention. I didn't want to be recognised. But the message was too important to walk away from.

I could see myself on the box sitting across from the host Waleed. It was a surreal moment. I was so sad. I guess that made sense because my best friend had passed away a fortnight before. I was still a mess trying to cope day by day with my devastation. There I was on screen talking about the past two years of my life...

Ash: When you go to a protest, it's kind of like being at a rock concert. The adrenaline is unbelievable. We thought it was like the beginning of Nazi Germany again and Victoria Police were the Gestapo. I truly believed that we we're headed towards a police state.

Waleed: It's a crazy concept, but one Ash says she truly believed in because at the time she had nothing else to believe in. She had lost her job, her freedom and over time, her will to live. How lonely would you say you were feeling at that time?

Ash: At points, probably suicidal.

Waleed: Ash supported lockdowns at first but confronted with a tidal wave of misinformation online, she quickly changed her mind.

Ash: I was sitting there sixteen hours a day, just on the internet, doing my research and I started believing it. At the time I just thought I was fighting for the freedom of Australia.

Waleed: Ash, who is transgender, says being part of the freedom movement made her feel accepted. What did you like about these people?

Ash: There is a lot of love in that community, a lot of misinformation. which I didn't realise at the time. People coming up to me, giving me hugs and adding me on Facebook. I felt like I was important. But when you're reading that much information and you're at the protest calling the police every name and then you're barricading your door because you think the police and ASIO are after you, it becomes stressful. It just consumes your whole life in a very unhealthy way.

Waleed: Ash says her family didn't support her views, so she cut ties with them. She saw the other protesters as her brothers and sisters until they abandoned her one day.

Ash: The police were say 100 metres away walking towards us. I go, OK, we're going to stand our ground. What they're doing isn't ethical and I'm marching with my flag and I turn around and they all had buggered off.

Waleed: All the other protesters?

Ash: Yeah. including one of the leaders.

Waleed: Ash decided to cooperate with the police. They didn't arrest her, just told her to go home.

Ash: The police rock up at my door a few days later, six of them. Normally I'd get up and say "F--- Off" and slam the door and stuff and I kind of gave it up. They were treating me very well. They're like "We've got families too, and we don't necessarily want to be at the protest, but our job is law enforcement".

Waleed: Over the following weeks, police dropped over to Ash's place a few times.

Ash: I was blown away that they'd come just to check up on me. These people are kind of treating me better than some of the leaders of the protest movement did.

Waleed: Ash says the fog around her head began to clear. Her feelings changed from anger to guilt.

Ash: I consider myself that I was brainwashed, but a lot of that was also my fault. The way I treated authorities and the things I wrote on the internet, I feel really ashamed, and I want to put this part of my life to bed.

Waleed: Since she's left the movement, Ash has reconciled with her family, been vaccinated and started a Masters Degree in music. Her true passion. But putting this chapter of her life behind her hasn't been easy. Ash says she's received death threats from protesters. Do you feel scared?

Ash: I feel cautious, not scared. I'm more concerned for my family.

Waleed: So in what way?

Ash: I hope they don't, you know, take it out on them in any way. I own this. This is my mistake. Part of me is glad I went through it because I probably would have necked myself if I didn't find some sort of community, but yeah there's just so much shame involved. I find it hard to smile to be honest.

Waleed: Do you think you'll ever be able to forgive yourself or move passed that feeling of shame?

Ash: Yeah things are looking more positive for me. As much as I know that what some of the protesters are doing isn't 100% right, I still care about some of them.

Waleed: Do you think that those of us in society looking at the protesters and kind of being dismissive and scornful of them, do you think we're making a mistake?

Ash: Yeah, I think there needs to be a little bit more understanding that they're human beings. Right or wrong, that's what they believe, and they deserve a little bit more compassion.

STUDIO COMMENTARY AFTER THE SEGMENT:
Gosh, that desire to be connected and to be part of something is such a strong desire. And you can see how quickly it happens. You think of your phone, and how quickly the algorithm changes, and then you start getting fed all the same information, and before you know it, that is the truth, that you're the truth because you're not seeing anything else. So it was a matter of weeks. Yeah. It was extraordinary how fast that happened. I've heard a lot about the idea that it's like a rock concert. Like looking at the Canberra convoy that feels like a festival almost. Like, they're sharing food, they're taking care of each other, they're singing songs together, there's this other side to it that most of us don't understand. Yeah and I feel that the point that's so important is the point at the end about listening to each other and I think when you stand and yell at people, either way, no one's going to take being yelled at and say "Yeah, good point". So it's a matter of listening to each other. She just wanted people to listen to each other.

I got calls from friends and family saying how well it was presented and I felt proud that I dared to follow through that far, all the while knowing the backlash was going to be severe. I got recognised several times on the street over the next few weeks but it was all positive comments, except the trolls online that would amount to thousands of negative comments, yet not one of them about what I did, it was all about what I was. I screen-captured some of their comments and forwarded them to their friends list so maybe some of them received a nice little dose of karma...

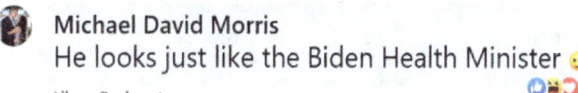

Michael David Morris
He looks just like the Biden Health Minister 😉
Like   Reply   1 w   👍❤️😆 8

Tasos Papadopoulos
Michael David Morris Twin sister...or should I say brother? 😆
Like   Reply   1 w   🤣 1

Troy Tempest
wow just looked at pic un relised who it is seen her before a shill she/he is a man in diffrent guises on here but the face u cannot change
                                                     👍 7

Angela Cadwallen
Not even going to give them a click. This bloke obviously has all sorts of issues and would be the last person I would be taking advice from in regards to the freedom movement. I was in a cult once, the Catholic Church, I think I can tell the difference!
Like   Reply   1 w   👍 5

Karyn Shalagin
She?
Like   Reply   1 w   👍 3

Des Tan
Karyn Shalagin it's a trans
Like   Reply   1 w   👍 2

Mel Ann · Follow
I find it pretty alarming the amount of people that have to resort to insults about gender in the comments.

So much for 'freedom'

These sorts of derogatory remarks are absolutely not necessary.

You can pick and pull a part so many contradictory statements in this interview and make your point without resorting to petty insults.

Your lack of ability to do so just demonstrates how incapable you are of articulating your point.

2y Like Reply   13

 Robert Troisi
I'd be interested to know if Ash was paid for this so-called interview. They slipped in how bad these protests are, promoted the police, and pushed vaccinations. That so-called interviewer should stick to comedy.

2y Like Reply   16

 Oskar Bock
Main stream media always interview the hot chick's. They're taking advantage of her beauty..

2y Like Reply   6

    Alex Nómad
   Oskar Bock her???
   2y Like Reply 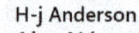 4

       H-j Anderson
      Alex Nómad - exactly what I was thinking too 🫣
      2y Like Reply

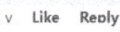 **Marjie Spies**
I watched the interview, this person used to spend I think it was 16 hours a day watching conspiracy videos!
Disgusting, biased "journalism". Absolute BS and exploitation of her. But I'm sure she got a nice paycheck from channel 10.

2y Like Reply   20

CHAPTER 17

THE FALLOUT

Speaking of assholes, Rukshan Fernando (aka Real Rukshan) being a very ordinary citizen journalist, did a video reply to my segment on The Project and he was trying to bait me as the troll he is. So I rose to the occasion and took the bait to reply to his lack of journalistic integrity and research to do a live online video with Lucky Lance and tore Rukshan a new one. Here is that extract courtesy of Lance:

Ash: So the real Rukshan, I'm giving him the courtesy of calling him by his professional name, which he didn't give me in his video. He just kept referring to me as a "certain individual" a "certain person" and never named me once. So my integrity is a lot higher than his and so I'll be referring to him as "Rukshan" or "Real Rukshan" because I'm not going to stoop that low.

Lance: He doesn't have any integrity so you're wrong there. He doesn't have any level of integrity.

Ash: That's what I mean, but I have some.

Lance: Yes, you do.

Ash: So I want to reply to a couple of things that he said and also there were a couple of important questions that some of his followers asked. One of his followers asked how much I paid, I'm a shill and I'm doing this for money. I can tell you now that I got paid nothing. I wasn't offered anything from any of the media that I've done since The Age, the ABC, The Project, whatever. And even if they did offer me money, I wouldn't have taken it ... Okay, I got paid on last Friday, and I have that much left after my bills. (showing on screen around $30 cash) So yeah, I need it... but my integrity, I couldn't do it.

Lance: So categorically, you weren't paid, you didn't ask to be paid, you weren't offered to be paid and making money was a furthest thing from your mind. You just wanted to tell your story, your experience in the movement. So that's that debate.

Ash: Yeah, I think that's nipped in the butt now. They can go and contact Channel 10 or whatever they need to do and they'll get the same answer. One of the things Rukshan said, again, I bring up on referring to his name, not calling him a certain individual, is he kept saying that I was distributing at protests a radical extremist pamphlet which is made up. I've never done such a thing. The only thing remotely even close to that concept would be I was writing a novel set in the dystopian future and there was a chapter on counter tactics against police. That kind of shows you the lies that he says. His followers just believe it straight away. That's not the case at all. I've never distributed anything at any protest except giving people hugs.

Lance: Well, I've met a lot of journalists in the last two years. And what I've been shocked when it comes to journalists, I've rang journalists and said, I've got a story for you. This person in the movement has done this, which is, whether it's fraudulent, illegal, whatever it is. And every time they're like, oh, now we can't go to print on that if we can't verify it. And I think I've got really good proof. They're like, now we need more verification, we can't go to print without stronger verification of the facts. And I had a big shock. I was quite shocked. I was like, wow, I didn't know that so many people in media had this type of integrity. Because some people in the media do tell lies sometimes. They have about me in the past. But anyway, I was shocked that in general, all the journalists that I've spoken to on the phone in the last two years, their level of integrity is high. Whereas with Rukshan, he's not a journalist, he's heard third hand from a "cooker" that you were handing out pamphlets. And he just puts that into his story as fact. Now, one very important fact, I don't know if you were gonna say this, but if Rukshan was a journalist, we wouldn't be having this conversation because you would be putting a complaint to the press council and they would force him to make a retraction. Right?

Ash: Another comment he said that if he felt and he said it's quite evident that I've been exploited by Waleed and The Project and I'm a depressed individual with all these problems and whatever he was saying. I wasn't exploited at all. They treated me well and were very compassionate with the story and I thought they did quite a balanced story showing compassion on both sides.

Lance: Exactly. It was simply a person giving an honest story of your experience in the movement. You just told your story. You had nothing to hide. You had nothing to gain. You had no motivation to embellish or exaggerate. It was just a simple interview of you telling your story and you were quite nice. You didn't use rude words or you didn't insult anyone. You just simply gave your take on your experience in the movement, that's all that was. And Rukshan has come out and tried to make it out to be something else.

Ash: But that should show you something as well by me doing that, the bi-product of it is that they're worried because they know that movement is in its last stages. It's starting to unravel, they're starting to implode, turn on each other and create new angles. They know the game is up. We're going back to our normal society slowly, but we're getting there. They expected us to already be in a police state and when I was in that brainwashed cult of idealism, I thought the same thing. This is the last point anyway. I've copped many thousands of comments and I've read a few of them. To be honest, I'm quite thick-skinned. And of course, when you read it, it's not enjoyable, but it kind of gives me a chuckle because every single one of them is attacking me personally about being transgender. They're so insecure about their movement and cause that they can't discredit anything that I said on The Project or anything in print, so I thought that was quite interesting and quite telling of that movement because they're quite right-winged and they're not fans of the LGBT community.

Lance: Yeah, well, he's pretty quiet on acknowledging the fact that there are Nazis in the protest. He likes to avoid that.

Ash: Even though he had a picture with good old Neil Erickson. Well, that's the thing, it has been infiltrated. When I was in it, there was no talk like that and no "Peacemakers". They were just sort of a thing starting up with Nick Patterson and after I left I noticed the violence did increase quite significantly to the point where they're smashing police officers out and throwing flares and all that stuff. It kind of makes me wonder because there's just so much evidence against their narrative. Do they truly think that the worldwide *media, all the governments, all the leaders, absolutely billions of us have conspired just to make COVID up? Even when I was brainwashed I kind of thought "Oh okay maybe COVID might be a more severe version of the flu or more contagious" but I've had it...you've had it. I can tell you it's frickin real it hits you like a freight train and if you aren't vaxxed then that freight train might continue to derail.,,*

CHAPTER 18

HATE CRIME

I have been fairly harsh on occasion to some of the people in the anti-everything movement and sometimes probably a bit too harsh. A documentary called "Battleground Melbourne" came out around this time, documenting the protest movement and the hard-line enforced by Victoria Police during the lockdown. Initially, I didn't even watch it all and jumped on the bandwagon and bagged it out, but a year or so after its release I sat down with an open mind and empathy and, although I don't agree with some of the opinions, I must say that Topher Field, the director, did make a good documentation of things that happened while we were locked down. I wrote to him apologising for my strong words and also praising him on a job well done and he appreciated that.

Around the middle of 2022, the television show "Sixty Minutes" reported on the neo-nazi movement in Australia with an undercover reporter infiltrating it over several months with a hidden camera. It was interesting to see that some of those faces were people I had seen marching with the anti-lockdown protesters . I couldn't believe it how police protected them during their rallies where they did the nazi salute at an anti-transgender protest, a protest organised by the same anti-lockdown movement. And then counter-protesters got arrested for disturbing the peace while these scumbags get an escort from the cops to and from their cars.

As far as my involvement went I was done with everything regarding protesting, but I also was pleased that I had accomplished something that may help others and myself, it was time to ignore the haters and move on. Besides I was only a few days away from returning to full-time study and beginning my Masters Degree. I only got to attend one class because, as to be expected, being trans means you are in fear for your safety every single day.

I knew it had to happen at some point. For the most part, living in St. Kilda is a great place for anyone in the trans community, but it honestly is all just an illusion. I cop crap every single day whether it is mild such as being misgendered or some drunken wanker along Fitzroy Street yelling "Hey everyone that's a bloke!". You develop a thick skin and it just becomes part of daily life. It's much worse in the outer suburbs but St.Kilda, always renowned for its openness to the LGBTQ community, is known for having the occasional nutcase or two and on March 8th of 2022 I met one through a violent assault...a hate crime!

I had met this person named Aaron Johnson at my apartment block. He was the son of one of the tenants named Nicky. She was a lovely lady and over the first few months since I moved in there we had grown to become good neighbourly friends. Aaron visited once and I sat out in the common area with him and a small group of other tenants over a beer or two. The next day I went to put my rubbish out into the collection bins and he made some comment to me calling me a fairy. I ignored it but his mother Nicky didn't. She kicked him out immediately and I thought that to be very admirable and a testament to her character. Of course, she will always love her son but that kind of behavior has no place in modern society especially in the usually quite accepting community of St. Kilda. I thought nothing more of it and never thought I would encounter him again.

That following Tuesday morning at around 2am I was on a writing spree and decided to refresh my brain and go to the 7-Eleven along Fitzroy Street for a cappuccino. I rarely drink any form of coffee but I wanted to put in a few serious hours into this book, the one you are reading now. As I left with my coffee someone about thirty meters away started yelling out insults such as faggot, poofter and "love your shoes, where can I get some?" and I ignored it. I crossed the road onto the back lane of my street and the idiot was still going on.

Now I have always lived my life by something Billy Joel once said: "Don't take shit from anybody", so I yelled back "Fuck You". I wouldn't change a thing regarding my comeback and I would do it again tomorrow without any fear. His reply was "I will be seeing you tomorrow then" obviously about him knowing where I lived. I replied "Why wait until tomorrow, come and say what you need to say right now" and so he briskly trotted across the road and we were face to face. His eyes were wide open, glassy and I imagine he was probably on crystal meth as well as being extremely drunk. I told him CCTV was everywhere so if you want to do something then go ahead. His insults continued and I told him to find something original because I hear that every day. I had my cappuccino in my hand with the lid sitting barely on and considered throwing the boiling beverage into his face. By now I felt threatened and pre-emptive self-defense would have been justified. I knew if he went for a swing and a typical headlock like most fights do, then I would be fine and just dislocate his shoulder while escaping his headlock, muck around with his pressure points, or blind him with my fingernails. If his swing/punch connected then I would be in immediate trouble but I was confident this guy was spending the next few nights in hospital if he wanted to proceed.

We slowly backed up and I thought my bluff had worked as we began to walk our separate ways. As I slightly turned he king-hit me (known in Australia as a coward punch) from behind. I fell and tried to regain my bearings but he followed it up punching me while I was on the ground several times. He then choked me in a sleeper hold position and I blacked out briefly. The last thing I felt was a kick in the head and I knew I was in serious trouble.

I stumbled to my block of flats and knocked on Nicky's door. I was bleeding profusely and she promptly called the police and ambulance. Police detectives arrived as well as paramedics and photos and statements were taken before I was whisked away in an ambulance heading to the Alfred hospital with a broken jaw, my teeth out of alignment and a hefty concussion. I was extremely lucky to be alive because I happened to fall on a garden bed and not the hard ground. Detectives visited me the next day in the hospital and informed me that he had been caught and taken into custody. My recovery was long and horrible as I had two steel plates and four bolts attached to my left jaw to keep it together. Even as I write this many months later I still get daily dizzy spells and I am now suffering PTSD with horrific nightmares.

My jaw was swollen for several months and had to be drained every week because of a complication during surgery which made my saliva glands automatically fill up too much. I was fortunate enough that the job I was supposed to begin the week after my assault was held for me while I recovered. A group of anti-scamming activists organised a "Go Fund Me" campaign and I received some donations which helped me get through the next couple of months. Thanks to Joel Hill and Lucky Lance for their amazing support in arranging such a generous and legitimate crowdfunding campaign for me. An article was published about the assault in "Star Observer" by Shibu Thomas about a week later. I had no idea it existed until someone brought it into the local pub to show me. Here are excerpts from that article:

A Melbourne-based trans woman, who left the anti-vax movement in Australia, was the victim of a transphobic attack last week. Ash Jackson had recently gone public with her journey into the "freedom" movement and her decision to quit the group.

"A week ago, (Jackson) was the target of an unprovoked trans-hate assault where she was king hit five times, choked unconscious, and kicked in the head, resulting in a severely broken jaw requiring surgery and dental work," said Joel Hill, who set up the GoFundMe campaign on behalf of Jackson. "The offender is on remand and is known to be violent to other women, including putting his mother in a coma a few years ago. He also stole $800 of Ash's rent money, which the police were unable to locate," the campaign page revealed.

The page posted photos of Jackson after the attack. "Surgery is required, and it's a specialist surgery which will result in a long time of recovery where she can't work or do much of anything at all," the campaign page added. Jackson had last month told The Age that she was "brainwashed" by the freedom movement – a disparate group of anti-vaxxers, right-wing activists and QAnon followers united in their opposition to masks, lockdowns, and COVID-19 vaccines.

Each Friday I would have to visit the hospital and have a few syringes of saliva and other disgusting liquids removed, only to have the swelling return within a few hours. The last resort was having a specialist inject Botox at the same time as syringing out the mess of fluids. This process took about an hour and was extremely painful but it finally solved the issue and the next week I did my first shift as a bartender at a concert venue called MEMO, while Paul Kelly and Archie Roach played on the stage. MEMO is like a smaller version of the Palais just across the road and has world-class acts from Australia and abroad. Some of the artists that have played there include Ross Wilson, BABBA, Wilbur Wilde, 1927, The Black Sorrows, Don Walker, Jon Stevens, Debra Byrne, Lindsay Field, Robben Ford, Electric Mary, Angus Burchell, Brett Garsed, my musical idol Jack Jones and some sensational tribute artists.

The PTSD from my attack affects me every day but it was quite intense around that time. Anyone on a tram that looked dodgy instantly was an panic trigger and even any slight chance of a confrontation would cause me to sometimes break down. My only solace was that the offender was in custody and I had been hoping for a very long sentence. The way the police portrayed it was that as a hate crime, he would be facing several years, alongside the amount of time someone would get for attempted murder. They had a zero-tolerance approach, but it's too bad the courts did not think the same way.

In late September after three adjournments Aaron pled guilty which I was relieved about. The police dropped several of the charges and left him with only one: Recklessly Causing Injury. I couldn't believe it... I was the victim of a violent hate crime that could have killed me and to my disbelief the judge released him on the spot for time already served. The only consolation was the very strict probation conditions. The judge read out my victim impact statement which listed my physical and psychological injuries. I finished it with "I forgive you Aaron and I hope that in time you can find a way of accepting people that are different like me. Perhaps through education...It's never too late to change".

Ironically the "never too late" line was of course said to me over a year earlier at the Box Hill Police station and a tiny part of me felt that I needed to pass it along. I still walk the street very cautiously and in fear that the probability of getting assaulted or killed is almost a guarantee at some future point. I was disgusted to find out that Victims of Crime compensation in Victoria is capped at $1200 and it's a long process just to get that. So if you got bashed and paralyzed or turned into a vegetable through a criminal act, yes your total payout for compensation is a maximum of $1200...forget about what you saw in the "Chopper" movie where people were getting $5000 in the 1980s, that no longer exists and it is a tortuously long journey just to get anything currently through the tribunal that governs all claims.

The nightmares of my whole life continue every single night when I sleep. The most recurring ones revolve around gangs trying to break into my parents' home and I cannot keep up with closing the doors and windows so eventually I fight them and I wake up usually with my leg is kicking the wall next to my bed. Another one is my family disowning me and I'm begging and crying to them but I have been cut out of the family. Also, the time I hit my father is recreated in my nightmares. I never have a peaceful dream or good night's sleep, I just have constant nightmares and stop breathing multiple times from sleep apnea. That combined with the prospect that I am guaranteed to get dementia later in life thanks to so many concussions, means I have no plans for any long-term future at all.

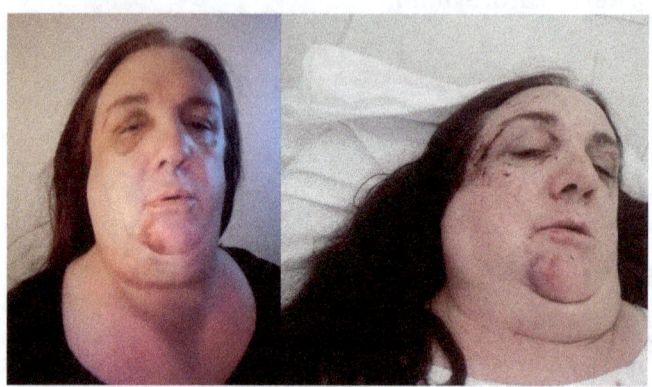

The result of my assault

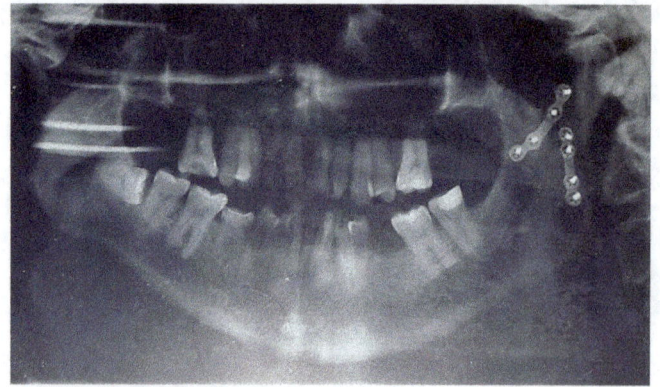

Aaron Johnson served around 200 days on remand

CHAPTER 19

FINAL THOUGHTS

It only took just over three decades to finally meet the biggest musical influence of my life in person. My former bandmate Steve Howie, from Exploded View, and I went off to "Lucky13" in Moorabbin to see a gig by Jack Jones with his band that had two members from the original Southern Sons band: Guitarist and the flavour of the band Peter "Reggie" Bowman and the energy and killer bass grooves of Geoff Cain. It was also the first time Steve had seen me as my true self and we were excited to see such an awesome bunch of talented musicians. The venue was on the small side with about 200 in the audience. It was great to see them all together on stage and what a sensational gig it was.

I still can't get over how someone can sing that well and play guitar at an equally high level and he was playing at that standard in his late teens decades ago. He always has the most smooth guitar sound and his style is melodic but he can tear the fretboard up with the best of them too. When he sings "Hold Me In Your Arms" there is a note he hits at the end of the bridge section and I swear it goes on for thirty or so seconds while he gradually brings in vibrato.

After the show, I went outside to say hello to Geoff and he remembered that gig at the Universal Theatre so many years ago. I asked if it is possible to talk to Irwin (Jack's real name) and he said you might catch him around in the car park but he does like to leave fairly quickly sometimes. I walked around the corner and saw him loading up his gear into his car. I didn't want to spook him out as some crazy fan so I said: "Irwin, it's Ash from MEMO music hall". I started dropping names of promoters from MEMO and also his manager's name, who ironically was Steve's cousin. He greeted me graciously and I told him I had been wanting to meet him for over thirty years. Then we had a brief chat about guitars and he said it was lovely to meet me and gave me a hug. Thank you Jack, and thank you Southern Sons...

Steve Howie (my drummer) and I meeting Jack

I thought it would be important to write about my family because they are everything to me even though I disappoint them more times than even they would care to count. I would lay my life down without any second thought for any of them and I love them beyond any words I could write, but I shall give it a go. My Mum is my best friend and is such a gentle and caring person. She only sees the good in all people and there's not a nasty bone in her body. I have no idea if I will be able to cope when she passes. The same as with my Dad. He is a gentleman and quite reserved emotionally but will go out of his way to do anything for others. Always the centre of attention in a group, a natural-born leader and bloody good singer too.

My brother Brad is married to Francesca and they have three gorgeous girls. The eldest Alice just turned fifteen which makes me wonder where the time went so quickly. Mary is the middle child and I'm pretty sure it's safe to say she is a genius. Pandora is the youngest and a very cheeky girl, but all three are immensely talented dancers and musicians. I'm so proud of them and would do anything for them. I have put my whole family through a lot and I keep making mistakes, but I am trying to better myself. I wish I got to see them more often but not having a car or license makes it very difficult. I adore my family x

The year 2023 had its ups and downs and as I sit here writing I am not sure why but I started cutting myself again and a lot more savagely. The scars on my arms are now visible and quite distressing to look at so I try my best to cover them up with makeup. I know it's the result of not keeping on top in managing my borderline issues combined with everyday drinking to excess, but I don't think any more counseling is going to help me until I am truly ready to receive it. The last two that I saw I walked out of after about twenty minutes as I knew every single thing they were about to say. I think I am beyond help. Something inside me died years ago and I just don't love myself enough to care. My life is a cautionary story about how to completely achieve no career, no relationship and no self-love. How can I ever love another person if I don't love myself?

Earlier in the year I turned fifty and had a big party. Over the previous few years, I had made my community of friends and it was an absolute honour that they all showed up. We had met at the local RSL and Bowls club usually centred around playing games of pool, a game of "chess on felt" that has taken me many years even just to be an average player, again thank you to Brad... My party was great but it was spoiled when we went over to an after-party and my drink got spiked and I was a mess for several days.

I thought I was finally on my way to finding happiness but having gender dysphoria and never being able to afford any corrective surgeries to ease it means I am hanging on by a thread all the time. I have so many health issues and my guitar-playing days are numbered due to nagging injuries starting to return. I also just got diagnosed with Macular Degeneration so if I make it to sixty I will be well on my way to becoming blind. I guess there is always a tiny part of me that still sees hope, but I look back on my life and think: What a waste! Hopefully I can play in a band again one day. Hopefully I can get gender reassignment surgery if this book sells. Hopefully I can someday find a balance in life with self-love. There is always hope.

As a transgender woman who lives 24/7 and all the flack that comes from that, I am still very unsure about the new so-called "trans community" which has somewhat hijacked the legitimate purpose of people like me who just want to try our best to fit in, have a job and make friends which hopefully will end with a happy-a-life as possible. And I'm not saying "only trans that are 24/7 are the real deal". We all start somewhere part-time either at home or having the courage to go out in public and it's a timeline that is different for everyone.

The community has branched off into so many confusing factions that in all honesty it has set it back 20 or 30 years, pissed the general public off and all because it was pushed too much on society way too fast. Pronouns like "they" and "them" are something even I am trying to get used to and understand because I feel like a female and always have, but others are blurring the very lines that are the fabric of everyday life and all "they" are doing is making it more dangerous for me to fit into general society and I should know better than anyone, as a victim, how violent that can be.

In saying all this, I have tried my best to educate myself and show compassion, but if I'm at the local women's help centre and someone walks in in a floral dress and a beard like Santa Claus, then yes that affects my life because they are taking the piss in deciding not to be one or the other: male or female. I am going to be ostracised from the community for these comments but I think in ten years that won't even matter because society is not, and probably never will be, ready to accept a third non-binary gender or variations of that. If I am wrong then I shall be the first to admit it and will retract everything, but for now I am really disillusioned by the whole transgender movement which has become more of a broader term encapsulating everything that has very little to do with my daily life, except it affects it greatly...

It's a hard life for anyone to transition, especially the older generation that seems to have been through a lot more roadblocks in life. I'm not saying that younger people transitioning today would be a walk in the park by any means, but there was just too much shame involved for me to go through it at an earlier age. Transitioning before the horrendous effects of male puberty is life-saving and even transitioning after going through that, while still being young, can make such a difference to "passing" as a female.

There are way too many internet influencers now that have ruined any further progress for the transgender movement. They come across as "taking the piss out of women". Dylan Mulvaney pointing to her crotch and saying "It's time we normalise the bulge" and buying tampons and documenting her "Days of Girlhood" as she transitioned and acted like a little infant girl, did nothing but frustrate a society that was just starting to get used to everyday trans people. Other people claiming "I identify as a thirteen-year-old girl" (but they are actually fifty), or others claiming they can "get pregnant and have monthly periods" is ludicrous, and I have no time for such nonsense. No you are not transgender, you are mentally ill, far worse than I could ever be.

Others like Jeffrey Marsh come off as creepy saying things directed at children like "If you have no one to talk to about your gender journey, join my Patreon page and we can chat privately", plus again taking the piss by dressing feminine but not shaving off his facial three-day growth. You are the reason I am in fear for my life every day. No wonder bigots like Matt Walsh go on so much about how they want the transgender community wiped off the face of the Earth. That is not an understatement. If I was in America I would probably have been murdered by now, especially in the southern states.

Some might say I have a slightly right-wing attitude to the

transgender issue but I don't consider myself right, left or even "woke". To quote Ricky Gervais: "If woke still means what is used to mean: You're aware of your own privilidge, you try to maximise equality, minimise oppression, be anti-racist, anti-sexist etc, then YES I am definitely woke... If woke now means: Being a puritanical, authoritarian bully who gets people fired for an honest opinion or even a fact, then NO I'm not woke. Fuck that!"

I will never pass as a woman, there is just too much damage done from decades of testosterone running through my disgusting body. All I can do is try my best to cope with the crap I cop every day and hang onto those people that embrace me as my true self. There is hope out there I guess. I'm finally going back into serious songwriting again and forming my own band soon.

Mental health is such a devastating condition and as we grow older the baggage of life becomes heavier and heavier. I guess there might be light at the end of the tunnel and I certainly plan to stick around to find it, but for now, that path is slightly grey...

I remember watching an interview with magician Jeff McBride and he said: "A dream is a goal with a deadline". That always resonated with me and got me through the completion of many things in my life, including this book. Something that I want to thank you, the reader, for allowing me to take up moments of "your life" by listening to the story of "my life". Writing a memoir is not something I would easily recommend anyone to go through, it's a gruelling process that affects your every day life. I am by no means an author in any way, I honestly have read less than ten books in my entire life. I'm not sure if this read is a good one, but it has been a difficult one and it's not over yet. All I can do, all anyone can do is hope...

My first wedding as myself My dear friend Laura

Lucky Lance dropping into to my 50th birthday party

My 50th birthday celebrations with family & friends

www.ingramcontent.com/pod-product-compliance
Lightning Source LLC
Chambersburg PA
CBHW071908290426
44110CB00013B/1324